don't burn your fingers

hula-hoop action

come into the parlour said the spider to the fly

Hookorama

Rachael Matthews

MQP

MQ Publications Limited

12 The Ivories, 6–8 Northampton Street

London N1 2HY

Tel: +44 (0) 20 7359 2244

Fax: +44 (0) 20 7359 1616

49 West 24th Street, 8th Floor

New York, NY 10010, USA

Tel: 212-223-6320

email: mail@mqpublications.com

www.mqpublications.com

EDITOR: Katy Bevan

PHOTOGRAPHY: Angus Leadley Brown

DESIGN: C-B Design

ISBN (10)   1-84601-107-8
ISBN (13)   978-1-84601-107-8

Printed and bound in Europe

1 2 3 4 5 08 07 06 05 04

Contents

Yarn foreword

Crochet, that most dainty of pastimes, conjures up images of Victorian gentlewomen intent in their mission to cover everything in the drawing room with little lacy whimsies. I remember my childhood fascination with all things haberdashery, entering our dark and dusty local store to be served by equally dusty ladies, where I purchased the finest steel crochet hooks and the finest cotton (no. 60 I believe), to crochet the finest pair of wedding gloves or a doily with coloured flowers. Then, yes, there were the afghans – blankets for charity or waistcoats made from patchwork squares of coloured wools – followed by a more free-form mode of ragbag stripy tank tops or flowers to decorate the hair. It couldn't have been simpler – just a hook and a loop of yarn and you were off! Circles and spirals, leaves and petals, a lacy shawl, a floppy hat or a bag – you can make anything with crochet. Learn the basic stitches – chain, double crochet

and treble – and you can be creating little sculptures by turning in all directions, or building spirals by working many stitches into one, as well as making wonderful accessories and fashions. Admittedly, crochet developed an unfortunate image in fashion terms, in the design hell that was the 1970s, but surely it's time to forgive and forget? Look carefully and you will see crochet in evidence in many designer collections in beautiful filigree patterning or bold statements from Yohji Yamamoto to John Rocha, Jean Paul Gaultier to Prada. If you are a beginner, this book will show you how, with fun projects to inspire your own creations. If you're really adventurous there are many other delights to discover within and beyond *Hookorama*, wherever your imagination leads. Crochet can be as varied as each individual and has an inimitable style all its own. Enjoy!

Sandy Black

Reader in Knitwear and Fashion
London College of Fashion
University of the Arts, London

Go forth and crochet

Welcome to the loopy world of crochet! We have loved making this book and we hope you will enjoy making these projects, but don't feel restricted to these particular patterns. Take inspiration from these antics and make your own fabulous creations! There'll be no stopping you.

In the process of writing this introduction, I thought it would be a good idea to find out the history of crochet, so that we can be aware of our own importance in its history, as we crochet heirlooms and pass on our skills to our friends and family. I discovered endless claims about who invented it, and where and why. Many cultures have claimed crochet as their own for thousands of years. At some point in our evolution, people started picking up sticks, knocking a notch in one end, and hooking loops to provide practical solutions to keeping warm, then inventing beautiful patterns to decorate and celebrate life. So in the beginning, a long, long time ago, there was a slipstitch. As with knitting, the craft was done on journeys, in the home, and for the love of civilisation.

I was taught knitting before I learned how to crochet. Knitting and crochet are quite different but go well together to give you more freedom to make what you want. The trance you can build up with crochet is just as good as the one you get with knitting, if not better. The action of crochet has a different tempo. Knitting has two needles, which dance together in a flicking action. Stitches fly from one needle to the other, as your yarn is entwined around a finger, which acts as a shuttle, creating new loops as old loops slip down into the rows of your beautiful creation. Stitches can be twisted in cables and you can switch your mind into pixel mode as you intarsia. The action can be furious, with needle points clicking together, needle ends gently tapping the arm of the person next to you on the bus, row counters creeping upwards, and calculations in your head as you complete your rows.

Watch the way your hands move when you crochet and the action is quite different. There is only one hook and the other hand is responsible for the tension. The tension hand holds the yarn in a triangle while the hook

Louise fell hopelessly in love with the wig, but Annie got to wear it to the ball.

dances around the thread in fluid, circular movements, with the hook picking up stitches wherever you want to go. You can work in circles, in squares, or any shape you wish, working backwards, forwards, inside out, and around things. You can imagine yourself drawing, adding a bit here, picking up a bit there. Crochet is started with chains, which can move into two or three dimensions and any other dimension you can think of.

After all your busy crochet action, there is only ever one loop left on your hook. This means you are free to pull your hook out at any time and play with your work. It will unravel but there are no dropped stitches! The hook can also be used to join pieces together and embroider chains, so you rarely need to thread a needle.

Crochet has different applications from knitting. As I became familiar with the craft, I suddenly started to notice there are blank edges everywhere you look, which can be jollied along with pretty borders. Frame the electric switches, make flowers for your windowsill and put new edges on last year's clothes. Crochet can be very practical but it is also about decoration.

As in knitting, the possibilities are endless and we work into the night and never want to go to sleep. I feel it is only fair to warn you of the dangers of crochet. Once you start it is very difficult to stop. This is a craft made up of loops and rounds and the same thing can happen to your mind. The focus can be so strong that you become sleep-deprived, hungry and dehydrated. Set an alarm clock to remind you of your everyday routine, and if you remember, take deep breaths and stretch regularly.

Above all, be very proud of what you have made. Even if it doesn't come out quite as you imagined, creativity is all part of a journey through life where we pick up new skills, solve problems, realise ideas and have a lot of fun and satisfaction. Happy hooking to you all.

Rachael

This is Rachael ready for any hooking emergency in her homespun hat.

all set for a stylish holiday

sunshine and shade parasol style

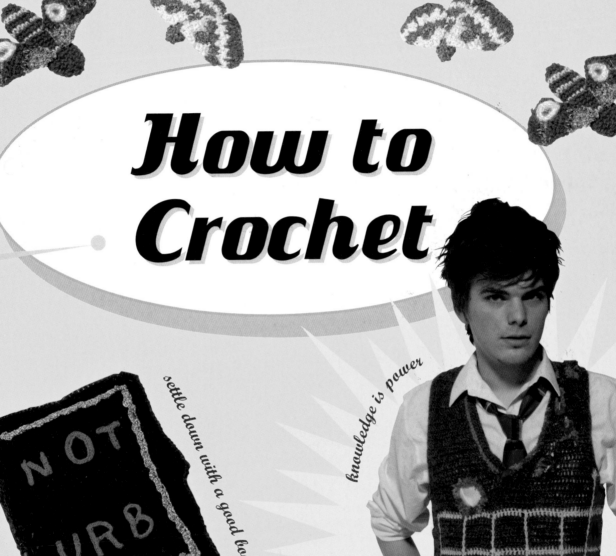

How to Crochet

settle down with a good book

knowledge is power

NOT
URB

Tools for the job

Hooks are lovely to collect as, somehow being single, they are more endearing than knitting needles and can have lots of character. You can put them behind your ear, just like you do with a pencil, or carry one in your top pocket in case of emergencies.

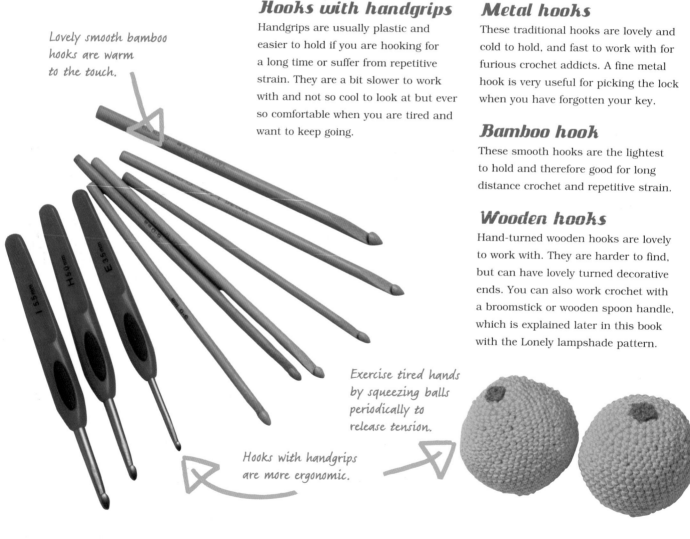

Lovely smooth bamboo hooks are warm to the touch.

Hooks with handgrips

Handgrips are usually plastic and easier to hold if you are hooking for a long time or suffer from repetitive strain. They are a bit slower to work with and not so cool to look at but ever so comfortable when you are tired and want to keep going.

Metal hooks

These traditional hooks are lovely and cold to hold, and fast to work with for furious crochet addicts. A fine metal hook is very useful for picking the lock when you have forgotten your key.

Bamboo hook

These smooth hooks are the lightest to hold and therefore good for long distance crochet and repetitive strain.

Wooden hooks

Hand-turned wooden hooks are lovely to work with. They are harder to find, but can have lovely turned decorative ends. You can also work crochet with a broomstick or wooden spoon handle, which is explained later in this book with the Lonely lampshade pattern.

Exercise tired hands by squeezing balls periodically to release tension.

Hooks with handgrips are more ergonomic.

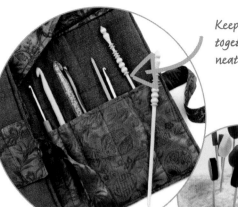

Keep your hooks together in a neat pouch.

Don't let anyone pinch your scissors.

Antique hooks

Old hooks appear all over the place if you look hard enough and they are a joy to collect. You can find them in second-hand shops, at the bottom of tool-boxes, and in among the knitting needles. If you are lucky you might find an ebony or ivory one. Modern hooks are measured in millimetres but the old hooks had numbers. There is a size conversion chart at the back of this book to help you identify them.

Scissors

Every crafter needs their own scissors. Make sure you get them back when you lend them out because people use scissors for all the wrong reasons! Tools for cutting yarn and fabric should only be used for that. Don't let a flatmate use them for opening cartons or trimming fingernails – they will be ruined and never cut well again. Tie a colourful ribbon around the handle so you can find them easily.

Tape measure

These are ever so useful and you can wear them as a neck tie while you are working. Some tape measures have little rivetted holes in so you can pin them to a tailor's dummy, or the sofa.

A radio or stereo

Music really helps a working atmosphere. Fluent knitters are able to watch TV and knit at the same time but crochet demands a bit more concentration and looking. I like to hire audio books from the library, or download podcasts. A good chat with a friend is the best tool of all.

Hand cream

Not everyone needs hand cream but if you do have dry hands, it can be helpful, or I suggest you work with pure wool and oil your hands with lanolin... lovely.

Vintage hooks are a joy to behold.

How to get hooking

The basics of crochet are very simple. Once you have made a basic chain you are well on your way, as even the most complicated and decorative stitches are just variations on this simple stitch. These instructions are all for a right-handed person. If you are left-handed, look at the step images in a mirror and they should show you the correct way to do the stitch.

Holding the hook and yarn

To crochet successfully it is important to hold the yarn and hook in a correct and comfortable manner. This will ensure that the gauge is accurate and consistent throughout your chosen project. There are many individual ways of holding the hook and yarn in crochet and it may feel awkward at first. Here are just two examples – choose whichever variation seems to come naturally to you.

Put these moths in your stash to fend off the real thing.

Holding the hook

* Hold the hook in your right hand as you would a knife. (Make sure that you don't hurt yourself.)

* Hold the hook in your right hand as you would a pencil. (Think about what you are going to make, rather than what you might write.)

Holding the yarn

Wrap the ball end of the yarn around the little finger of your left hand, passing it under the third and middle finger and over the forefinger, using your forefinger to create tension.

✱ Wrap the ball end of the yarn around little finger of left hand, passing it over the other three fingers. Hold the work steady with your thumb and forefinger and use the middle finger to create the tension.

Make a slipknot

1 Make a loop in the yarn. With your hook, catch the ball end of the yarn and draw through the loop.

2 Pull firmly on yarn and hook to tighten knot and create your first loop.

In the beginning was the slipknot...

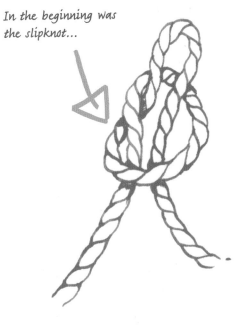

Making a chain (ch)

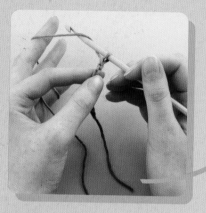

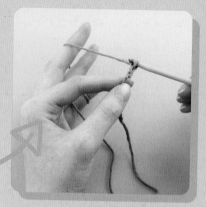

1 To make a chain, hold the tail end of yarn with the left hand and bring the yarn over hook (yoh) by passing hook in front of the yarn, under and around it.

2 Keeping the tension in yarn taut, draw the hook and yarn through the loop.

3 Pull the yarn and hook through the hole and begin again, ensuring that the stitches are fairly loose. Repeat to make the number of chain required. As the chain lengthens keep hold of the bottom edge to maintain the tension.

How to count a chain

This is how you count the chains to know if you have got enough.

To count the stitches, use the right side of the chain, or the side that has more visible and less twisted 'v' shapes.

1 Don't count the original slip stitch, but count each 'v' as one chain.

TIP
As with all crochet, have the ball on your left if you are right-handed. Find a way to wrap the yarn around your fingers, so that you keep them relaxed and not clinging on to the yarn.

Make a slip stitch (sl st)

A slip stitch is used to join one stitch to another or a stitch to another point, as in joining a circle, and is usually made by picking up two strands of a stitch. However, where it is worked into the starting chain, only pick up the back loop, as shown here.

1 Insert the hook into the back loop of the next stitch and pass yarn over hook (yoh), as in chain stitch embroidery.

2 Draw yarn through both loops on stitch and repeat. Going back over the row like this makes a strong and useful chain.

Stephen won't spill his hot chocolate because he has a non-slip coaster.

TIP
Keep calm when you are learning and drink some relaxing hot chocolate, not that strong espresso, to help keep a steady hand.

Double crochet (dc)

Here you can see that the hook is passed through the whole stitch (two strands). We have given you drawings as well as photographs here as they are sometimes easier to follow.

1 Insert hook, front to back into next stitch; two strands and one loop on hook. Yoh.

2 Draw through to front; two loops on hook.

3 Draw through both loops to complete double crochet.

4 The finished stitch should look like this (see fig 3). Work one dc into every stitch to end.

Double crochet

1

Yarn pulls through the first loop only at this stage.

2

It ends up looking a bit like this hopefully.

3

Yarn goes through both stitches at the second stage.

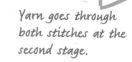

Half treble crochet (htr)

This is a popular stitch that makes a firm fabric.

1 Start by putting the yarn over the hook (yoh).

2 Insert hook in next stitch, from front to back and draw through the stitch only.

3 This creates three loops on the hook.

4 Yoh and draw yarn through three remaining loops on hook together to complete htr.

Keep your crochet fingers warm between rows.

Treble crochet (tr)

This makes a more open fabric. The stitch is called a treble in the UK because of the three moves to make the stitch.

1 Wrap the yarn over the hook (yoh) from back to front so there are two loops on the hook.

2 Insert hook in next stitch, from front to back. Yoh and draw through stitch.

3 Three loops on hook. Yoh and pull through two loops.

You don't have to be a schoolboy to learn new things, so keep reading.

4 There are two loops on the hook. Now put the yarn over again (yoh).

5 Pull through remaining two loops to complete treble (tr).

Double treble crochet (dtr)

You will need a turning chain of four to reach the height of this elongated stitch.

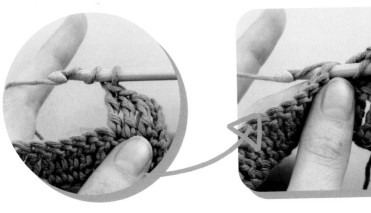

1 Wrap yarn round hook twice (yoh twice).

2 Insert hook into next stitch, yoh and prepare to pull through.

3 Pull yarn through stitch to front, four loops on hook, yoh.

4 Draw yarn through two loops, leaving three loops on hook. Yoh again.

5 Draw yarn through two loops, leaving two loops on hook, yoh.

6 Pull yarn through both remaining loops to complete double treble (dtr).

Triple treble (trtr)

This stitch combines a double and a treble together to make a fabric with tall posts.

1 Wind yarn round hook three times (yoh three times).

2 Insert hook into next stitch, yoh and pull through stitch to front.

3 Five loops on hook, yoh and pull through two loops.

4 Four loops on hook, yoh and pull through two loops.

5 Three loops on hook, yoh and pull through two loops.

6 Two loops on hook, yoh and pull through all remaining loops on hook to complete trtr.

What to do at the end of a row

At the end of a row, when you turn the work to begin the next, you need to complete a turning chain to get to the right height of the stitch you are working. This chain counts as the first stitch in the row and each technique, depending on its height, uses a different number of chain stitches at the start of the row.

Is it the last stitch of a row, or the first stitch of the next row? The jury is still out.

1 After completing a row, turn work. Make turning chain in the same way as a normal chain. Yoh.

2 Draw yarn through loop on hook and repeat to height of chain required (see table below).

Turning chain table

Type of stitch	Chain stitches
double crochet	1
half treble	2
treble crochet	3
double treble	4
triple treble	5

Mask making is a bit like drawing on make-up and is a very creative pastime.

Round in circles

There are two ways to begin circular crochet – with a chain or a loop. Once you have chosen one of these ways to start, you just keep going round and round.

Making a yarn loop

This way of working in the round ensures that there is no hole in the middle of the work, as there is with a chain ring.

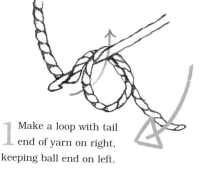

1 Make a loop with tail end of yarn on right, keeping ball end on left.

2 Pull ball end through loop (you will need to steady work with hand).

3 Make one chain through loop on hook you have drawn through to steady the circle.

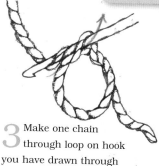

4 Work as many dc or whatever stitch you are using into the loop as required by pattern.

Making a chain ring

1 Work a chain as long as required by the pattern or the thickness of the yarn.

2 Join last chain to first with a slip stitch. Begin first round by working into each chain stitch.

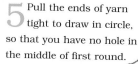

5 Pull the ends of yarn tight to draw in circle, so that you have no hole in the middle of first round.

Circular crochet

Working in rounds as opposed to rows means the last stitch of each round is joined by a slip stitch to the first stitch and the work continues as such, round and round, with no turning. This means it is easy to lose which row you are on and stitch markers are a good idea to remind you of where you started. To create a flat circle, rather than a tube, you will need to increase in every row. Work two stitches into each chain in the first row, then every other stitch in the following row, every third stitch in the third row, and so on. At the beginning of each round it is still necessary to make the turning chain, even though you are not actually turning the work, otherwise you will go round in a spiral creating a less even shape.

1 To join in a new colour, fasten off first colour and make a slipknot on your hook. Insert hook from front to back in stitch where you wish to begin new colour. Draw the hook through to front. Make chain to get work to height of stitch used.

2 Insert hook into next stitch and work stitch required by pattern. Continue to work round until you reach the beginning of round, which you may have marked with a stitch marker. Join round with sl st to top of first chain.

Going round and round can make you dizzy

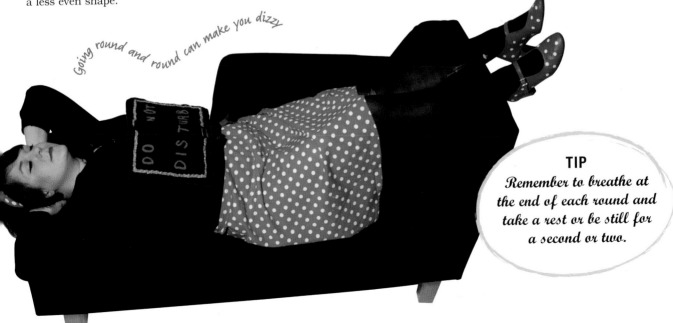

TIP
Remember to breathe at the end of each round and take a rest or be still for a second or two.

Tunisian crochet

Tunisian crochet is almost like a mixture of knitting and crochet. It is worked, like crochet, on a single hook, but the hook is long enough to build up loops on it, like knitting.

You always work with the right side of the fabric facing you. Firstly, loops are built up on the needle from right to left, then reduced down to one again by working left to right. The row is not fully finished until both of these actions have been completed – the second row is actually a completion of the first. The fabric is much firmer than knitting or crochet and the final look can resemble either. Work Tunisian crochet loosely as it has a tendency to produce a biased fabric with wavy edges.

Basic Tunisian stitch

1 Row 1: Insert hook into 2nd ch from hook, yoh, draw loop though and keep this loop on the hook. * Insert hook into next ch, yoh, draw loop through and keep this loop on the hook. Rep from * to end; do not turn.

2 Row 2: Working from left to right, yoh and draw a loop loosely through the first loop on hook, * yoh and draw through next 2 loops on hook, rep from * to end, until only working loop remains on hook. Do not turn.

3 Row 3: Working from right to left, miss first vertical, * insert hook from right to left under vertical loop of next st, yoh, draw loop through, keep loop on hook, rep from * to end. Do not turn. Row 4: As row 2. Rows 3 and 4 form pattern, ending always with a row 4.

Tunisian treble stitch

Make length of chain that will give amount of stitches required.

1 Row 1: Insert hook into 2nd ch from hook, yoh, draw loop though and keep this loop on the hook. * Insert hook into next ch, yoh, draw loop though and keep this loop on the hook. Rep from * to end; do not turn.

2 Row 2: Working from left to right, yoh and draw a loop loosely through the first loop on hook, * yoh and draw through next 2 loops on hook, rep from * to end, until only working loop remains on hook. Do not turn.

3 Row 3: Working from right to left, 1ch to count as first st, miss first vertical loop on front of fabric, *yoh, insert the hook from right to left under the vertical loop of next st, yoh and draw a loop through, yoh and draw through 2 loops on hook, rep from * to end. Do not turn. Row 4: as row 2. Rows 3 and 4 form pattern, ending always with a row 4.

This is what a Tunisian treble fabric looks like.

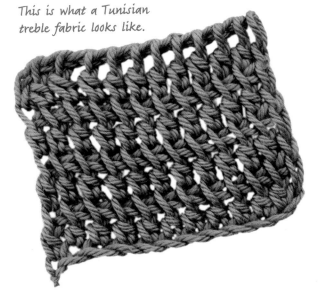

This banana skin is made with Tunisian crochet stitches.

Filet crochet

'Filet' means 'net' and filet crochet is basically a net, or mesh, with solid blocks forming shapes. Filet crochet is made up of chains and trebles – trebles worked in groups form the blocks while chains form the spaces. Patterns are usually worked from a chart.

Here's how

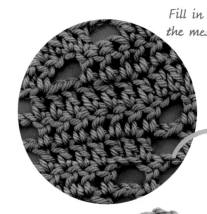

Fill in the holes in the mesh like this.

This is the basic filet mesh – you can fill in the holes to make patterns.

1 To make the basic filet mesh, make a length of chain with multiples of 3 plus 1, with an extra 4ch. Work 1tr into 8th ch from hook, the 7ch forming a 2ch space along the bottom edge, 3ch to count as first tr, with remaining 2ch, the 2ch space on row being worked.
* 2ch, miss 2ch, 1tr into next ch, rep from * along row. Turn.
Row 2: 5ch to count as first tr and ch sp, miss first tr, 1tr into next tr, *2ch, miss 2ch, 1tr into next ch, rep from * along row. Turn. These two rows form pattern.

2 To start a row with a block, make just three extra ch to count as first tr, work 2nd tr into 4th ch from hook, then work 2tr into each of next 2ch to complete block. To form spaces over blocks, work as you would work over a ch sp. 1tr into tr of previous row, 2ch, miss 2tr of block, 1tr into next tr.

Edgings

Crochet is perfect for producing neat and even decorative edgings. These edgings need not necessarily be restricted to crochet fabrics; they look just as interesting on knitting or loosely woven fabrics.

Corded edging

Join yarn to edge of work. Begin by working one row of dc evenly along the edge of work, being careful not to pull the work too tightly. Then work back along the row in dc, without turning work, from left to right. This is also known as crab stitch, or backwards double crochet and is used on the lampshade project (see page 126).

Shell edging

Join yarn to edge of work. Begin by working one row of dc evenly along the edge of work, being careful not to pull the work too tightly. Turn. Then work a slip stitch into first stitch *miss 2 sts, 5tr into next stitch, miss 2 sts, sl st into next stitch* repeat between stars for length of edge.

Picot edging

Use either with or without foundation row of dc, (example shows with). Then work 1dc into each of first three stitches. * 4ch, remove hook from last ch and insert in first of 4ch, pick up ch just dropped and draw through loop on hook to create picot, 1dc into each of next three stitches *, repeat between stars to end.

Shaping

Crochet is special in that you can stop in the middle of a row and make any shape that you want. You can increase and decrease in two-dimensions, or three-dimensions and any other dimension you can think of. This is very useful when you are making things that have a curvy shape, like oranges.

Oranges get bigger and smaller to make a nice round shape.

Increasing at the beginning of a row

1. Make a length of chain equal to the number of extra stitches required, minus one, plus the number of turning ch required for st being worked. Work across these sts as you would when using a starting ch, working into the ch which leaves the correct turning ch for st you are working.

2. Continue across the row as normal, remembering that the turning chain is now at the beginning of the increased stitches.

TIP
There aren't any rules, – you can increase and decrease whenever the mood takes you.

Increase at the end of a row

1 At the end of the row, pick up the final post of the last stitch and make another stitch here.

2 Continue in this way until the required number of stitches have been made.

Increasing in the middle of a row

1 To increase in the middle of a row, you work twice into the centre stitch. Use a stitch marker to help you identify which stitch to increase into on following rows. To create an even dart, alternate each row between increasing in the first or second of the increase stitches worked into the same stitch on the previous row.

Jennifer likes to keep her parasol closed indoors.

Decreasing

What goes out must come in again, and sometimes there are just too many stitches. You can relax a bit, as there is less action with decreasing: you just skip stitches and end up with less to do.

Decreasing at the beginning of a row

1 To decrease 1dc at beginning of row, make one turning ch, miss first dc, insert hook into next dc and draw loop through, insert hook into next dc and draw loop through, 3 loops on hook, yoh and draw through all three loops.

2 Work across the row until 2dc and turning ch remain. Decrease 1dc as at beginning of row, then work last dc into turning ch.

Little flowers increase in springtime.

Decreasing in the middle of a row

1 Work across to decrease position, decrease one over next 2 sts as given for the beginning of row. Use a stitch marker to mark the position of decrease.

2 To create a decrease dart, on each alternate row, work together the stitch before the decrease with the decrease st, then on the following row work the stitch after the decrease together with the decrease stitch.

Through both loops?

In early crochet, each stitch would have been worked strictly through the front of the stitch only, creating a significant difference between the front and the back of the work. These days it is more common to work through both loops, making the fabric more reversible.

This sample shows the texture created when the hook is pushed through both sides of the stitch.

This sample shows the texture that is made when only the front of the stitch is used (note the ribs on the back).

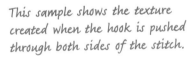

Colourful

In order to dye pure wool a more interesting colour, you need to wind it into a skein. However, hand-dyed yarns then need to be wound into a ball, or a bobbin for small amounts, to make them more manageable.

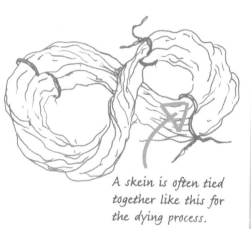

A skein is often tied together like this for the dying process.

Playing ball

Once you have a ball, not a skein, it is prone to rolling away. Make sure your ball of yarn can't escape and get spoiled, because you can guarantee that if there is a dark, dusty corner in your room where you can't quite reach, then that is where, with great speed and determination, your ball will roll. If you use your yarn from the end in the middle of the ball, then the ball will nestle happily beside you and it won't run away. (Some manufacturers make this easy and others produce balls that you have to disembowel to get at the end – there ought to be a

law against this.) If you wind your own balls from skeins then wind them around a thick stick – the Scandinavian term for this is a 'nostepinne' or winding stick – then you will find the end in the middle.

Bobbins and skeins

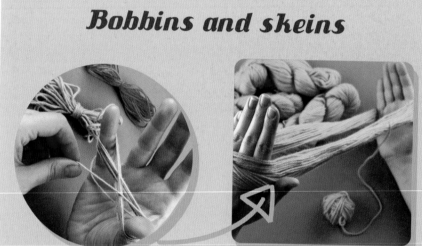

Winding a bobbin
Using your little finger and your thumb, wrap the yarn in a figure of eight. Kids like to do this as they learn a little song about it.

Winding a ball from a skein
Get a friend to hold the skein in their hands while you roll it into a ball. Put a nice tune on the radio and dance while you do this.

Don't end up in a big messy tangle like this.

Managing colour

To attach a new colour at the beginning or in the middle of a row, work the last stitch of the first colour until 2 loops remain on hook, draw new colour through these 2 loops to complete the stitch.

When the colours of yarn are changed many times in one row, the yarn not in use can be carried along the back of the work, until needed again. However, if wider areas of colour than about 3 or 4 sts are required, a separate ball, or bobbin, of yarn should be used for each shape.

On a right side row, yarn is carried along the back. With first colour A, *work number of stitches required, less one, and work this next stitch leaving the last 2 loops on hook, pick up B, carry over A and complete the stitch with B. Working with B, work number of stitches required, less one, and work this next stitch leaving the last 2 loops on hook, pick up A, carry over B and complete the stitch with A; rep from * across row, bringing in whatever colour is required in this way. On a wrong side row, the yarn has to be carried across the front of the fabric.

* Work number of stitches required for A, less one, and work this next stitch leaving the last 2 loops on hook, bring A to the front of the fabric and B to the back, completing the stitch with B. Working with B, work number of stitches required, less one, and work this next stitch leaving the last 2 loops on hook, bring B to the front of the fabric and A to the back, completing the stitch with A; rep from * across row, bringing in whatever colour is required in this way. Phew.

Here you can see the other colours carried along the back of the work as runners.

This is what it should look like on the right side, with no puckering.

Finished

Finishing is a very important part of crochet as it could make or break your project. The perfect join should be one you can't distinguish from the work, as bad finishing is always noticeable and messy.

As you come to the end of your project you can start planning the social event at which to introduce your newest creation. Your friends will be waiting with anticipation to see how it suits you. Don't let the side down by rushing to finish. Take an extra evening to check your seams, and try it on the next day in the clear light of morning.

Fastening off

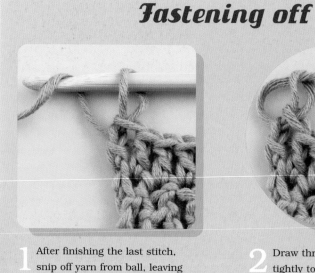

1 After finishing the last stitch, snip off yarn from ball, leaving about 20cm. Yoh.

2 Draw through tail, pulling tightly to fasten, leaving a long end to use for sewing up later.

Oooh look, her seams are unravelling, how shocking is that!

TIP
Always leave an end that is long enough to sew up your seams, as you might have run out of that yarn by the end.

Weaving in ends

1 Use hook to draw yarn through at least five stitches, winding the yarn over and under as you go to secure yarn and ensure it doesn't work free.

2 Snip off excess yarn.

Blocking and steaming

When you have fastened off and sewn or woven in all your loose ends, it is often a good idea to block your work. This gives you an opportunity to make sure that any garment pieces are the right size. Spray with a fine mist of water and press lightly, with a cloth over the work.

Novelty yarns and more textured work may not need blocking. In fact it may be a bad idea. Check the pattern and any instructions on the ball band before proceeding. A gentle spray and spreading the work out with your hands may suffice.

Slip stitch join

1 Place two pieces together, right sides facing. Work a row of slip stitch along the join, inserting hook through back loops only of both pieces (the two loops which touch when placed side-by-side).

TIP
We used contrasting coloured yarn so it would show up but if you don't want your seams to show, use the same colour as the main one.

Double crochet join

1 Place two pieces together, right sides facing. Work a row of dc where the two pieces join, going through the whole of both stitches.

Don't rush to finish, you may be using it for the rest of your life!

Whipstitch

1 Place two pieces together, right sides facing. Using a knitter's needle, join the back loops of each piece with a diagonal stitch motion.

It is always important to be properly finished.

Measuring gauge

Before starting on a project, it is advisable that you do a gauge swatch to ensure that you are crocheting at the right tension. This enables you to correct any deviations from the working pattern before you begin. The swatch should be just over 4 inches or 10cm square using the same stitch that is used in the pattern, or as indicated by the instructions. Knitter's pins are useful as the large heads won't disappear through the fabric.

TIP
Gauge swatches may seem boring but there are lots of things you can do with them afterwards.

1 Measure out four inches (10cm) along a row. Place markers.

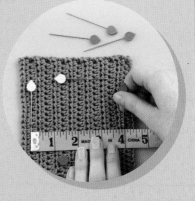

2 Measure out four inches (10cm) across the rows. Place markers. Use these two sets of markers to count how many stitches and rows there are to four inches (10cm) and compare to the gauge mentioned at the start of your pattern.

tea for two

Adam and Eve

a tasty little morsel

eat plenty of fruit

Fig-leaf bikini

Here is Mia in a fabulous creation, the fig-leaf bikini. The leaves are big, bold and beautiful for figure flattery, which is essential for Eve, as worries about one's figure do not do a girl any favours.

You will need...

YARN: Rowan Cotton Glacé,
100% cotton 115m/50g
3 balls 809 Pier
1 ball each 739 Dijon, 812 Ivy

HOOK: 3.5mm

Directions
Pants

FRONT: Ch56, 1htr in 3rd ch.

ROWS 1–6: 1htr into all to end, 2ch.

ROW 7: As row 1 but 1ch to turn.

ROW 8: Sl st 6sts, 1htr into each st to last 6sts, leave last 6sts unworked.

ROWS 9–12: 2htr tog, 1htr into each st to last 3st, 2htr tog, 1htr, 2ch to turn.

ROW 13: As row 9 but 1ch to turn.

ROW 14–15: Sl st 3, 1htr to last 3 sts leave last 3 unworked. Fasten off.

BACK AND GUSSET:

Ch76.

ROWS 1–6: 2ch, 1htr into 3rd from hook, 1htr into all to end. 2ch to turn.

ROW 7: As row 1 but 1ch to turn.

ROW 8: Sl st 5sts, 1htr to last 5sts that are left unworked. 2ch to turn.

ROWS 9–13: 2htr tog, 1htr into each st to last 3sts, 2htr tog, 1htr, 2ch.

ROW 14: 3htr tog, 1htr to last 4sts 3htr tog, 1htr, 2ch.

ROW 15: As row 9. **ROW 16:** As row 14. **ROW 17–18:** As row 15–16.

ROW 19–21: As row 15.

ROW 22: As row 14. **ROWS 23–27:** As row 15. **ROW 28–29:** As row 14. Keep working 1htr into all sts with 2ch as turning ch for 10 rows (this is the gusset). Fasten off.

MAKING UP

Sew the front, back and gusset together. Sew sides. Pick up all the stitches around leg, and 1dtr into all for an extra frilly look. Pick up all the sts around the waist, 1tr into each. Work in the round until it gets to about 6cm or the length you desire. Turn over and thread in elastic for a secure waist.

Bra

CUP (MAKE 2): Make 32ch.

ROW 1–3: 2ch, 1htr into the 3rd ch from hook, 1htr into each st to end. 2ch (turning).

ROW 4: 2htr tog, 1htr into each st, until last 3 sts, 2htr tog, 1htr into last st, 2ch.

ROW 5: 1htr to end, 2ch.

ROW 6: As row 4.

ROW 7: 1htr to end, 2ch.

ROW 8–9: As row 4.

ROW 10: 1 htr into all, 2ch.

ROW 11–13: 2htr tog, 1htr to last 3sts, 2htr tog, 1htr, 2ch. **ROW 14:** 1htr into all, 2ch. **ROW 15–16:** As row 11. **ROW 17:** 3htr tog, 1htr to last 4sts, 3htr tog, 1htr, 2ch.

ROW 18: As row 11. Fasten off.

BACK STRAPS:

Make 8ch, dc into 2nd from hook. Keep working in dc to end 2ch to turn, until the strap is long enough to reach all the way around you and tie in a bow at the back.

SHOULDER STRAPS:

Make as for back straps, ask a friend to help fit them.

Big fig leaf (make 2)

One fig leaf is made with 5 sections.

MAIN PART: 34ch, 1tr into 4th ch from hook. 1tr in every st to end.

ROW 1: 3ch. Turn. * Place marker on centre st.

ROW 2: 3tr into next st, 1tr into each st before marker. 1rftr (see page 52), 1tr into each st to last 2 sts. 3tr into next st, 1tr. Turn.

ROW 3: 3ch, 1tr into each to 3sts before marker, 3tr tog, 1rbtr, 3tr tog, 1tr into each st to end. Turn.

ROW 4: 3ch, 1tr into each st to 3sts before marker, 3sts tog, 1rftr, 3tr tog, 1tr to end.

ROWS 5–6: As row 3–4.

ROWS 7–14: 1tr into each st without decreasing but keep doing 1rftr and 1rbtr alternatively on the central st.

ROW 15: 3ch, 1tr into each st to 2sts before marker, 2tr tog, 1rftr, 2tr tog, 1tr into each st to end.

ROW 16: 3ch, 1tr into each st to end (with 1 rbtr in the middle).

ROW 17: 3ch, 1tr into each st to 3sts before marker, 3tr tog, 1rftr, 3tr tog, 1tr.

ROW 18: As row 17, with 1rbtr at centre. **ROW 19–20:** As row 17–18.

ROW 21: 1tr into all with 1rftr at centre.

ROW 22: 3ch, 3tr tog, 1tr. Fasten off.

SECOND PART (MAKE 2):

* The other side of leaf should be symmetrical. 8ch. 1tr into 4th ch from hook, 1tr into each st to end, place marker in centre stitch.

ROW 2: 3ch, 3tr into next st, 1rftr, 3tr into next, 1tr.

Making up

Sew the five parts of the leaf together.

Place the big leaf on the centre of the pants like this.

Attach two small leaves to the bikini top like this.

ROW 3: 3ch, 3tr into next, 1tr into each of next 2sts, 1rbtr, 1tr into next 2sts, 3tr into next, 1tr.

ROW 4: 3ch, 1tr into each st to end with 1rftr in the middle.

ROW 5: 3ch, 2tr into next st, 1tr into each of next 4sts, 1rbtr, 1tr into each st to last 2sts, 2tr into next, 1tr.

ROW 6: 1tr into all sts with 1 front raised st in centre, 3tr into last st.

ROW 7: 3ch, 1tr into each st to 3sts before central st, 3tr tog, 1rbtr, 3tr tog, 1tr into each st to end. Turn.

ROW 8: 3ch, 1tr into each st with 1 front raised tr in the middle.

ROW 9: 3ch, 1tr into each st to 2sts before central st, 2tr tog, 1rbtr, 2tr tog, 1tr into each st to end. Turn.

ROWS 10–14: 1tr into each st with 1rftr or 1rbtr alternatively at centre.

ROW 15: As row 9.

ROWS 16–20: As row 10.

ROW 21: As row 9.

ROW 22: 3ch, 1tr into next, 3tr tog , 1tr to end. Fasten off.

THIRD PART:

ROW 1: 6ch. 1tr into 4th ch from hook. 1tr in each st to end. Turn.

ROW 2: 3ch, 2tr into the st that has 3ch, 1rftr, 3tr into last st.

ROW 3: 3ch, 2tr into next, 1tr into next, 1rbtr, 1tr, 2tr into next, 1tr.

ROW 4: 3ch, 2tr into next, 1tr into

each of next 2sts, 1rftr, 1tr into each of 2sts, 1tr.

ROWS 5–8: 1tr into each st with 1rftr, or 1rbtr in the middle alternatively.

ROW 9: As row 5 but make 5 ch at end.

ROW 10: 1tr into 4th ch from hook, 1tr into each st to 2sts before centre, 2tr tog, 1rftr, 2tr tog, 1tr into each st.

ROW 11: 1tr into all sts but having 1rbtr at centre.

ROWS 12–14: As row 10.

ROW 15: 3tr tog, 1tr to last. Fasten off.

Small leaf (make 6)

MAIN PART: Ch24, 1tr into 4th ch from hook, 1tr into each st to end. Place marker on central st.

ROW 2: 3ch, 3tr into next, 1tr into each st to central st, 1rftr into the central st, 1tr in each to end.

ROW 3: 3ch, 1tr into each st to 3sts before central st, 3tr tog, 1 back raised tr, 3tr tog, 1tr into each to end.

ROW 4: As row 3, with 1rftr in centre.

ROWS 5–9: 3ch, 1tr into each st, with 1rftr, or 1rbtr in centre alternatively.

ROW 10–13: 3ch, 1tr into each st to 3 sts before central st, 3tr tog, 1rftr (or 1rbtr) 3tr tog, 1tr into each st.

ROWS 14–15: 3ch, 1tr into next, 3tr tog over next 3 tr, 1tr into each st to end. Fasten off.

SECOND PART (SYMMETRICAL):

6ch,1tr into 4th ch from hook.

ROW 2: 3ch, 2tr into the same st as chains. 1rftr. 3tr into the last st.

ROW 3: 3ch, 3tr into next st, 1tr, 1rbtr, 1tr, 3tr, 1tr.

ROW 4: 1tr into each st to end, with 1rftr in the middle, 6ch.

ROW 5: 1tr into each st to 2sts before the centre, 2tr tog, 1rbtr, 2tr tog, 1tr into each st to end.

ROW 6: 3ch, 1tr into each st, with 1rftr in centre.

ROW 7: As row 5. **ROW 8–9:** As row 6. **ROW 10:** As row 5. **ROW 11:** As row 6. **ROW 12:** 3ch, 1tr into next, 3 tr tog. Fasten off.

THIRD PART: Ch4, 1dc into 3rd ch from hook, 1dc into each st.

ROW 2: 3ch, 2tr into the same st as 3ch, 1rftr, 3tr into next.

ROW 3: 3ch, 2tr into next, 1tr, 1 rbtr, 1tr 2tr into next, 1tr into next, 5ch, turn.

ROW 4: 1tr into 5th ch from hook, 1tr into each of next st, 2tr tog, 1 rftr, 2tr tog, 1tr into each st to end.

ROW 5: 1tr into each st (1rbtr in centre).

ROW 6: 3ch, 1tr into each of next 2st, 2tr tog, 1rftr, 2tr tog, 1tr, turn.

ROW 7: 3ch, 3tr tog, 1tr into each st.

ROW 8: 3ch, 1tr into next, 3 tr tog. Fasten off.

The Garden of Eden

Here are Cast Off members Mia and Jo dressed as Adam and Eve. The Garden of Eden was the first place of colour, texture, inspiration and temptation. Today you can only visit gardens like this on the spring bank holiday, but you can have a similar experience in your local yarn store all year round.

Grapes Directions

2DC CLUSTER: Put hook in next st, yo, pull through loop – 2 loops. Put hook in next st, yo and pull through, yo and pull through all 3sts. Ch2 leaving a 10cm tail.

You will need...

YARN: Rowan Cotton Glace 100% cotton 115m/50g
1 ball each in 815 Excite, 823 Damson, 746 Nightshade, 787 Hyacinth, 812 Ivy
Sirdar Silky Look DK 93% acrylic 7% nylon, 135m/50g, 964 Mulberry and oddments of other purple DK or 4ply yarns. Glittery yarns make the grapes look washed and ready to eat. Can also be made in shades of green.

HOOK: 2mm hook

RND 1: 4dc in 2nd ch from hook.
RND 2: 2dc in each dc (8sts). Tip: do not join rounds with a sl st, just keep crocheting around.
RND 3: 1dc in nxt dc, 2dc in nxt dc,* rep from * to * around (12sts). Now give the tail you crocheted over a good tug – this will draw the stitches together into a little cone. Drop the tail and don't crochet it with the stitches any more – it will now act as a marker for the beginning of the round.

ROUNDS 4–6: 1dc in each dc (12sts).
RND 7: 1dc in next st, 2dc cluster over next 2sts * rep from * to * around (8sts). Now stuff the grape – a great moment to recycle old tights, rags, bits of wool, other yarn or fleece gathered from barbed wire fences (washed and dried thoroughly). The blunt end of a crochet hook is a great stuffing tool.
RND 8: 2dc cluster over next 2sts around (4sts). Skip next st, sl st in next st. Fasten off and thread tail of yarn onto needle and weave in and out of top to secure opening.
MAKING UP: Using green yarn make ch to length required, then sl st up and down, making branches off as you go. Sew the grapes into clusters and attach to stem.

This lush bunch of grapes is made with four different purples to add depth and magic.

Blackberry leaf
Directions
Raised front double treble (rfdtr)

Yoh twice, insert hook from the front around stem of st below from right to left, then complete treble in the usual way.

Raised back double treble (rbdtr)

Yoh twice, insert hook from the back around stem of st below from right to left, then complete double tr in the usual way.

You will need...

YARN: Rowan Cotton Glace 100% cotton 115m/50g 812 Ivy, 739 Dijon

HOOK: 2.5mm

FOUNDATION CH: 14ch, make stalk as foll: 1 sl st in 2nd ch from hook, 1 sl st in each of next 6ch, make 9ch more.

ROW 1: 2tr in 4th ch from hook, 1tr in each of next 2ch, 3tr tog over next 3ch, 1dtr) in next ch (at top of stalk), 3tr tog over next 3ch, 1tr in each of next ch, 3tr in last ch. Turn.

ROW 2: 3ch, 2tr in first tr, 1tr in each of next 2tr, 3tr tog over next 3sts. 1 rbdtr around stem of dtr, 3tr tog over next 3sts, 1tr in each of next 2tr, 3tr in 3rd of 3ch. Turn.

ROW 3: 3ch, skip first tr, 1tr in each of next 2tr, 3tr tog over next 3sts, 1rfdtr around stem of rbdtr on previous row, 3tr tog over next 3sts, 1tr in each of next 2tr,1tr in 3rd of 3ch. Turn.

ROW 4: 3ch, skip first tr, 3tr tog over next 3sts,1 rbdtr around stem of rfdtr, 3tr tog over next 3sts, 1tr in 3rd of 3ch. Turn.

ROW 5: 3ch, work next 4sts tog (1tr in next st, 1rfdtr around stem of rbdtr, 1tr in next st and 1tr in 3rd of 3ch). Fasten off.

Simple 4-petal flower

With 2mm hook and 4-ply off-white cotton, 6ch and join in ring with sl st. * In ring 3ch, 3tr tog, 3ch, sl st to ring. Rep from * to complete four petals. Fasten off.

You can never have too many leaves. When it is autumn, make them in orange and red.

The Poppy
Directions

Ch 5 and join in ring with sl st. 12dc into ring and join to first dc with a sl st. * 3ch, 2dc into first dc, 3dc into each of next 3dc, sl st to next dc. Repeat from * to complete three petals.

CENTRE: With 2mm hook and 4-ply navy or almost black cotton, 4ch, sl st into ring, 10dc in ring, 1dc in each dc, 1dc, miss l st, 1dc. Fasten off and draw up to close into a button and attach to centre of flower.

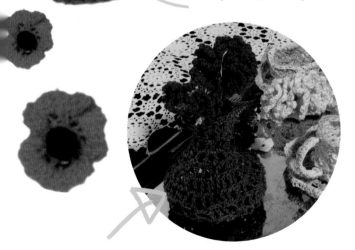

Records of poppy cultivation go back to 5000BC in Mesopotamia, between the rivers Tigris and Euphrates, possibly the scene of the Garden of Eden.

Carnations are great for weddings, funerals, barmitzvahs and petrol stations (for vase pattern see our internet site).

You will need...

YARN: Oddments of 4-ply yarn in 2 colours, plus green

HOOK: 2mm or smaller than usually used for yarn

Carnations in crochet
Directions

Make Carnations in solid colours, red, pink or white, or in a pale colour with either a red or pink trim.

TO MAKE THE FLOWER HEAD: with main colour 4-ply yarn ch5 and sl st into a ring. 1ch and 9dc into ring (10sts), sl st to first dc.

NEXT RND: 1ch, 1dc into first dc, 2 dc into next dc. Change to 3mm hook. 2ch, 6tr into first dc, 7tr into each of next dc, join to first tr with sl st.

PICOT EDGE: Use 2.5mm hook and CC 1ch, * dc in next dc, ch3, sl st to first ch, dc in next dc. Rep from * around edge and sl st to first ch.

TO MAKE UP: Fasten off leaving a long tail, thread tail on to a darning needle and weave in end down to base of flower. Thread yarn in and out of base, bunching up petals and securing.

STEMS: With 2.5mm hook and green yarn ch50. Sl st into 2nd ch from hook, sl st 14. Make side branch/leaf as foll: * ch9, sl st 2nd ch from hook, sl st 7 then sl st to main stem. ** Continue sl st up the stem, sl st 7 then sl st to opposite side of stem make another leaf from * to **. Continue up the stem making branches/leaves on alternative sides of stem until four have been made. Sl st to top of stem.

MAKE A BUD: Ch then pull loop about 2cm tall, * yoh then into ch below, yoh and pull through ch. Rep from * until there are 7 loops on hook. Yoh and pull through all 7 loops. To make top of flower stalk: ch2, 9dc into 2nd ch from hook. Fasten off.

Lily of the valley

The legend of the lily of the valley is that it sprang from Eve's tears when she was kicked out of the Garden of Eden. It also means the return of happiness, sweetness and purity of heart, and protection from evil spirits in the month of May! Mia, however, protects our studio from evil spirits all year round.

You will need...

YARN: Rowan Cotton Glacé, 100% cotton, 115m/50g
1 x 50g ball 812 Ivy, 1 x 50g ball 725 Ecru

HOOKS: 2mm, 2.5mm, 3mm

Directions

FLOWER: Using a 2mm hook and Ecru yarn, make 5ch and sl st to first ch to make ring, 1ch (this turning chain counts as 1dc) 9dc in ring.

NEXT RND: 1ch (counts as 1dc), *1dc into next dc, 2dc into next dc. Rep from * for this rnd and join to first stitch with sl st.

These pretty bell flowers will make a lovely headress.

NEXT RND: 1ch * 1dc in next dc, miss next dc, rep from * for this rnd and join to first stitch with an sl st.

NEXT 2 RNDS: 1ch, 1dc in each and every dc and join to first stitch with an sl st.

NEXT RND(PICOT EDGE): 1ch (counts as 1dc), * sl st to next dc, 3ch, sl st to first of these ch, sl st to next dc, rep from * to complete rnd and sl st to first stitch. Fasten off

SMALL BUD/PARTLY UNFURLED FLOWER: Using a 2mm hook and Ecru yarn ch 5 and sl st to first ch to make ring.

FIRST RND: 1ch, 9dc into ring (10dc).

NEXT RND: 1ch (counts as 1dc), * 1dc into next dc, 2dc into next dc. Rep from * for this rnd and join to first st with a sl st.

NEXT 2 RNDS: 1ch (counts as 1dc) * 1dc in next dc, miss next dc, rep from * for this rnd and join to first st with sl st. Fasten off.

EXTRA SMALL BUD AT TOP OF STEM: Using a 2mm hook and Ecru yarn, make 5 ch and sl st to first ch to make ring. 1ch, 9dc into the ring (10sts).

NEXT RND: 1ch (counts as 1dc), 1dc in each of next 9dc, join to first st with sl st.

NEXT 2 RNDS: 1ch, * skip 1dc, 1dc into next dc; rep from * for this rnd and sl st to first st. Fasten off.

STEM: Using a 2.5 mm hook and Ivy yarn, ch70 – this is the main stem. Sl st into 2nd chain from hook, sl st into next 14chs. 10ch to side of main stem. Fasten off with a long tail. Thread tail of yarn through the centre of one of the flowers and pull through the chains/side stem and tie a knot in the chains to stop it from slipping out. Cut the yarn tail and knot the end to look like a stamen. Rejoin yarn to main stem and on the other side of the stem, rep from * above. Rejoin yarn to main stem and sl st next 10ch on main stem and rep from * to attach two more flowers.

MAKING UP: Create a stem and join another 2 flowers 10ch apart on one side of the stem only. Rejoin yarn to main stem and sl st next 10ch on main stem, then rep from * to attach two more flowers. Rejoin yarn and once again sl st to next 10ch but attach a larger bud in the same way as the last two flowers. Fasten off. This should leave a short part of the stem at the top that is made of single chains. Attach the smallest bud to the very end of these chains.

LARGE LEAF:

Using a 3mm hook and Ivy yarn, ch45. Sl st into 2nd ch from hook and into next 14ch.

* 3dc into each of next 3ch, 3htr into each of next 3ch, 3tr into each of next 3ch, 12dtr into each of next 12ch, 3tr into each of next 3ch, 3htr into each of next 3ch, 2dc into each of next 3ch, 1dc into last ch. 3ch, sl st to first ch from hook then working into the other side of last dc, rep from * working into the other side of chains worked for the first side of the leaf. Work another rnd around the outside of the leaf from * again and crossing over at the stem as before (making the same stitches as before except this time into the tops of previous stitches instead of into the chains). Sl st to next stitch and fasten off.

SMALL SPRIG:

Using a 2.5mm hook and Ivy, ch20. Sl st into 2nd chain from hook and sl st to next 9ch. Ch10 to side of main stem. Make two flowers and attach each flower to the top of each single chain stem. Thread tail of yarn through the centre of one of the flowers and pull through the chains/side stem and tie a knot in the chains to stop it from slipping out. Cut the yarn tail and knot the end to look like a stamen.

For authentic sweat and tears, Perspiration Gel is available from theatrical suppliers.

Serpents

Eden wouldn't be complete without a wicked serpent or two whispering temptations. It is a good job that Eve was good at listening otherwise we wouldn't know anything about life, and when it comes to crochet, a little knowledge goes a long way.

Maybe stuff your snake with small mammals and eggs?

You will need...

YARN: Colinette yarn: Giotto 50% cotton, 40% rayon, 10% nylon 144m/100g in colourways Venezia and Morocco

HOOK: 5mm

Directions
Space shell pattern snake

Make 4ch, join into circle with sl st, dc round increasing 1ch every 2dc till 24dc in total.

SHELL PATTERN:

RND 1: * 3ch, miss 3dc, 1dc into each of next 3dc repeat from * to last 3sts, 3ch.

RND 2: * (1tr, 3dtr, 1tr) into 3ch space, miss 1dc, 1dc into next st, repeat from *.

RND 3: * 1dc into each dtr, 3ch repeat from *.Repeat rows 2 and 3 till almost desired length.To shape tapered end * 1dc in next st, miss next st, repeat in rounds till 1st left. Fasten off.

TONGUE: Cut a piece of yarn about 30 cm long, make 10–20ch, wrapping both ends of yarn around hook. Fasten off. Embroider a couple of suitably beady eyes.

Solid shell pattern snake

Make 4ch, join into circle with sl st, dc round increasing 1dc every 2dc till 24dc in total.

SHELL PATTERN:

RND 1: Miss each of next 2dc, 5tr into 3rd dc, skip next 2dc, 1dc into next dc, rep from* around (24sts).

NEXT RND: * 1dc into 3rd of 5tr, miss 2sts, 5tr into next dc miss 2sts, rep these 2 rnds until the snake is almost the desired length. To taper end of tail, work shell pattern and continue thus:

RND 1: * 4tr into 1dc, 1dc into centre of 5tr, rep from *.

NEXT 4–5 RNDS: * 4tr into 1dc, 1dc into centre of 4tr, rep from *.

NEXT RND: * 3tr into 1dc, 1dc into centre of 4tr, rep from *.

NEXT 4–5 RNDS: * 3tr into 1dc, 1dc into centre of 3tr, rep from *.

NEXT RND: * 2tr into 1dc, 1dc into centre of 3tr, rep from *.

NEXT 4–5 RNDS: * 2tr into 1dc, 1dc into centre of 2tr, rep from *.

NEXT RND: * 1tr into 1st dc, 1dc into centre of 2tr, rep from *.

NEXT 4–5 RNDS: * 1tr into 1st dc, 1dc into centre of 1tr, rep from * fasten off and join up remaining dc.

Picnic time

I've learned that it's very important to be part of a tea set…to take tea with people who really inspire you, make you question the world you live in, and bring you plenty of joy. Here are Rosie and Harriet, questioning why these cups and saucers have been made with holes in them.

You will need...

YARN: Habu Textiles #: A-135, 100% ramie, 51m/28g
28g each of 0 (white), 1 (beige) and 3 (brown)

HOOK: 3.75mm

TIP
If you can't get hold of this yarn, try using DK and dipping in PVA to stiffen.

Ramie is made from a Chinese nettle-like grass, perfect for serving tea to the discerning picnic-goer.

Directions
Teaset

CUP

With MC ch6, join into a circle with sl st.

RND 1: Ch4, * 1tr in loop, 1ch, rep from * 7 times, sl st in 3rd ch.

RND 2: Next ch sp * 1tr, 1ch, 1tr, 1ch, rep from *.

RND 3: * Skip 2sp, 2tr, 1ch, 2tr in next sp, rep from * around sl st in top of 3 ch.

RND 4–10: Sl st into 1ch sp, 3ch, tr in same sp, 1ch, 2tr in same sp, in next 1ch sp, * 2tr, 1ch, 2tr, rep from * around, sl st in top of 3ch, fasten off.

With other colour yarn sl st in each st around top of cup. Fasten off.

HANDLE

With MC make 15ch, dc in 2nd ch from hook and in each ch with 3dc in end ch, work the other side of the initial chain in the same way. Fasten off.

SAUCER

With MC repeat rnd 1–2 of cup.

RND 3: * skip one sp, 2dc, 1ch, 2dc, repeat from*.

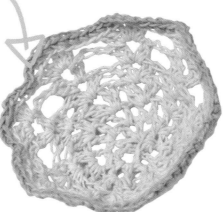

Daisy fascinator

In days gone by, a 'fascinator' was something that you had around your face to make you look 'fascinating'. Well here is the daisy version! This was constructed around a polystyrene head model, which is great for sticking pins in but you could find a friend who is prepared to sit still.

You will need...

YARN: Jaeger Trinity, 40% silk, 35% cotton, 25% polyamide 200m/50g
1 skein of each, Corn 430 (yarn A) and Cream 444 (yarn B), and Sage 431 (yarn C) for the vines and leaves

HOOK: 4mm

Directions

Start by making lots of daisies then make a vine that fits around the circumference of the head. Stitch into a ring. Then make a vine that reaches from front to back over the top of the head, and 2 or 3 from side to side, all stitched onto the circumference ring. This forms the basic structure and you can start to stitch the daisies and leaves on to this. Stitch the daisies to each other and to the vines. You can choose the shape of the overall effect. Make daisies as well as simple flowers and poppies from the Garden of Eden and grow your own hat.

Daisies

Using yarn A and 4mm hook, make 6ch and join in a ring with sl st.
RND 1: 1ch, 11dc into ring, join to first dc with a sl st (12sts).
RND 2: Join yarn B with a sl st to first dc * 12ch and join to next dc with a sl st, rep from * until end of round (12 loops/petals), join to first dc with a sl st. Fasten off.
LEAVES: With yarn C, make 7ch then 1dc into the 2nd loop from hook. 1htr into the next loop, 1tr into the next, 1htr into the next loop, 1dc into the last loop. Fasten off. This will make one tiny leaf. If you want two leaves all in one go, start from beg once more making 7ch from the same loop you did 1dc.
THE VINES: With yarn C start with slipknot on hook, * yoh and pull up a ¾ loop, (yarn over, insert hook in same st, pull up a ¾ loop) 3 times more, yoh and draw through all 9 loops on hook, ch1 * rep from *. Continue until vine fits around the head.

For long hair just keep adding more foliage! Whatever the weather you will look as fascinating as Amy

Pineapple handbag

Ancient folklore tells us that sailors would place a pineapple on their gateposts when they returned from a journey to let the friends and neighbours know they were home. We would miss Harriet if she ever left us so here she is with a Pineapple handbag she can't live without.

You will need...

YARN: Oddments of the following: organic-look yellow DK, Dark and medium green DK, Dark and medium brown DK

HOOK: 3mm

Realistic coloured yarn makes for an authentic-looking fruit.

Directions

MAIN PART (MAKE 3): With green yarn make 33ch to start.

ROW 1: Using green yarn, (3tr, 1ch, 3tr) in 5th ch from hook, skip 3ch, 1dc in next ch,* skip 3ch, (3tr, 1ch, 3tr) in next ch, skip 3ch, 1dc in next ch, rep from *, changing to yellow yarn at end, turn. Do not cut green yarn.

ROW 2: Using yellow yarn, 3ch, skip first dc, 3tr tog over next 3tr, * 7ch, skip 1ch, 6tr tog over next 6tr (leaving 1dc between groups unworked), rep from * ending 3tr tog over last 3tr, 1tr in 1ch, turn.

ROW 3: 3ch, skip first tr, 3tr in top of 3tr tog,* 1dc in 1ch space between trs 1 row below (enclosing centre of 7ch), (3tr, 1ch, 3tr) in top of 6tr tog, rep from * ending 3tr in top of 3tr tog, 1tr in 3rd of 3ch, changing to green yarn, turn. Do not cut yellow yarn.

ROW 4: Using yellow yarn, 4ch, skip first tr, * 6tr tog over next 6tr (leaving 1dc between groups unworked), 7ch, skip 1ch, rep from * ending 3ch, 1dc in 3rd of 3ch, turn.

ROW 5: 1ch, skip (first dc and 3ch), * (3tr ,1ch, 3tr) in top of 6tr tog, 1dc in 1ch space between trs 1 row below (enclosing centre of 7ch), rep from *, ending 1dc in first of 4ch, changing to green yarn, turn. Do not cut yellow yarn.

Repeat rows 2–5, changing colour every 2 rows until work is 17cm. Carry colours loosely up side edges of work. Sew three main parts together forming a tube for pineapple's body.

BASE: With brown yarn, pick up the stitches around the bottom of the pineapple. Work in rounds: 1dc into each stitch for 3 rnds.

RND 4: 1dc into first 5sts.

MAKE BOBBLE THUS: Insert hook into next st and pull out the yarn, yoh, insert hook into the same st, pull out the yarn, yoh, insert hook into the same st, pull out the yarn, yoh, pull through all loops on the hook. Work 1ch to complete.

Make bobbles randomly to make a bumpy pineapple skin on the bottom. Work 2 more rnds in brown yarn.

RND 7: 1dc into first 3sts, insert dark brown yarn. 1dc into next 4sts with dark brown yarn. Work 1dc into each stitch swapping yarn colour every 3 or 4sts, finishing this rnd with dark brown yarn.

RND 8: With dark brown yarn, * 1dc into first 10sts, skip 1. Rep from * to end.

RND 9: * 1dc into first 9sts, skip 1. Rep from * to end.

RND 10: * 1dc into first 8sts, skip 1. Rep from * to end. Fasten off.

CIRCLE AT THE BOTTOM: Make a yarn loop (see page 24), 5dc into the ring, joining them with sl st. Make 1ch to start.

RND 1: 2dc into all sts.

RND 2: 1dc into first st, 2dc into next st. Rep to end.

RND 3: 1dc into first 2st, 2dc into next st. Rep to end.

Follow this rule to make a circle, increasing the number of 1dc every rnd.

Keep working thus until your circle gets to the required size for the bottom. Sew this circle on to the bottom of the pineapple.

TOP: With brown yarn, pick up stitches all round from the second shells from the top. Work in dtr until your work measures more than 10cm.

LEAVES: With green cotton yarn, (need dark green and medium green) make 10ch. 1tr into the 4th ch from hook. 1tr into each ch, 3ch to start next row.

ROW 2: 1tr into first 2sts, 1rftr (tr round the stem you made in previous row), 1tr to end. Make 3ch.

ROW 3: 1tr into first 2sts, 1rbtr (tr round the stem but insert the hook from back side), 1tr to end. Make 3ch.

Repeat last 2 rows three times more, finishing with making 3ch. Start decreasing to make pointy bits:

How to construct a pineapple

Sew together the 3 body parts to make a tube.

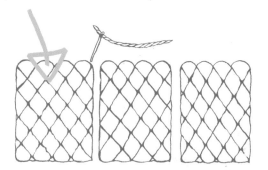

Pick up stitches and work from the top and bottom of the tube, sewing in the base.

Sew the leaves inside the top of the bag like this.

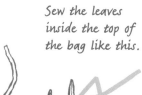

1tr into next 2sts, 3tr tog over next 3sts, 1tr into last 2sts, 3ch.

NEXT ROW: 1tr into each.

NEXT ROW: 1tr, 3tr together, 1tr. Fasten off.

HANDLE: Make 50cm ch, 1 dc into each the back of each ch.

Directions
Oranges are not the only fruit

You can use crocheted oranges for juggling, or as extra packing in your lunch box! Crocheted in pure cotton and stuffed with polyester stuffing, they are machine washable. A bouncy orange stuffed with a tennis ball makes a very acceptable gift.

Using orange yarn ch4, join into a ring with a sl st.

RND 1: Ch1, 4dc, in ring.

RND 2: 2dc, in each dc.

RND 3–6: 1dc, 2dc in next dc around (until about 48sts at end of rnd 6).

RND 7–16: 1dc in each dc.

RND 17: * 1dc in next st, 2dc cluster over next 2dc, rep from *.

RND 18: 1dc in each st.

RND 19: As rnd 17.

RND 20: As rnd 18. Stuff.

RND 21: As rnd 17.

RND 22: 2dc cluster over next 2dc, around (there should be about 8sts now).

RND 23–25: Dc in each st, sl st in first st. Fasten off.

For a bounceable fruit, stuff after round 16 with a tennis ball and carry on pattern, crocheting around the ball.

You will need...

YARN: For orange use Rowan cotton glacé 100% cotton 115m/50g. 1 ball 820 Pick & Mix or suitable colour plus oddment of green
For pomegranate use Colinette Lasso, 100% polyamide 205m/100g, in Fire 71

HOOK: Orange 2.5 mm, Pomegranate 4 mm

GREEN TOP FOR ORANGE

With the green yarn make a yarn loop, 5dc into the circle join with sl st. * 2ch, sl st into next dc. Rep from * to end. Fasten off leaving a long tail.

The pomegranate tree in the Garden of Eden symbolises 'the tree of life' and later the fruit became the symbol of eternal life.

keep active

too cool for school

Log Cabin Sexy

little Bo-Peep has lost her sheep

don't chip your fingernails

Herdwick hottie

This is a real sheep hot water bottle. The pure, hand-spun wool smells lovely when it gets hot, and keeps you warm all night while the sheep are sleeping out in the cold. This sheep is a Herdwick sheep with yarn from a farm near where I live. Herdwick wool is so full of goodness that if the sheep get stuck in a snow drift, they can eat their wool to survive, but I don't recommend it. The head is a flip-top head, which is secured by a loop around one eye, so you can fill the bottle easily.

You will need...

YARN: 3 shades of handspun Herdwick yarn, Aran weight, with one contrasting colour for the farmer's dye spot Habu Textiles #: A-135, 100% ramie, 51m/28g , oddment of 1 (beige), and 3 (brown) for the horns

HOOK: 6.5mm

MATERIALS: You will also need 1 hot water bottle

Directions

Start by making a chain that runs the length of your hot water bottle. This one started with 24ch.

ROW 1: Dc in 2nd ch from hook, dc to the end of the row, turn.

ROW 2: 1ch, insert your finger under both threads of dc, 1ch from hook. Now grab the yarn (with the hook) that is between your index and middle finger and pull it through the dc. You now have two loops on your hook, yo and pull through both loops *. Rep from * to * for next loop. You will place a loop in each dc. 1ch turn (see diagrams over the page for loop stitch).

ROW 3: 1dc in each dc across, 1ch turn. Rep rows 2 and 3 for desired length. Keep working in loop stitch, and play with the colouring of your sheep. The loops in loopy stitch all fall in the same direction, so it is better to make two sides of the bottle, rather than knit both sides in one go. Join up the side seams.

NOW MAKE THE HEAD: Sheep have different coloured faces, some light, some dark and some with patches. The choice of yarn is up to you. Make a chain to fit around the neck of the hot water bottle and join it with a sl st. Keep working up the head of the bottle in rounds of dc, increasing as you need, until you reach the top.

The head flips back for easy opening.

CONTINUED

NOW MAKE THE FLIP-TOP HEAD: Work around one side of the head, then make a ch the same length as the other side. Rejoin back into the rnd and continue upwards for about 4 more rnds. Start to decrease by skipping 1dc every 5dc. Continue until the stitches have diminished considerably, then stitch closed. This top part of the head needs to be stuffed with a little ball of wool to give it some shape.

Make a little ch around the opening of the head, long enough to reach around a button, which conveniently is also an eye. Stitch on the face in chain stitch – make it smile if you can.

THE HORNS (MAKE 2)

Using the ramie, which is quite horn-like, make a ring of 10ch, joined with a sl st. Work 3 rnds in dc. To make the horn curl, place two markers to distinguish one half of the round from the other half. One half will become a short side and the other a long side, which will make the horn curl. On the short side, pick up the stitches of the row below, making it gathered. On the long side, continue in dc. Keep going until you want to decrease the horn into a point. Do this by skipping a dc every few stitches. All horns seem to be different shapes, so you can have fun sculpting the shape you want. Stitch them on quite near the head.

Loop stitch

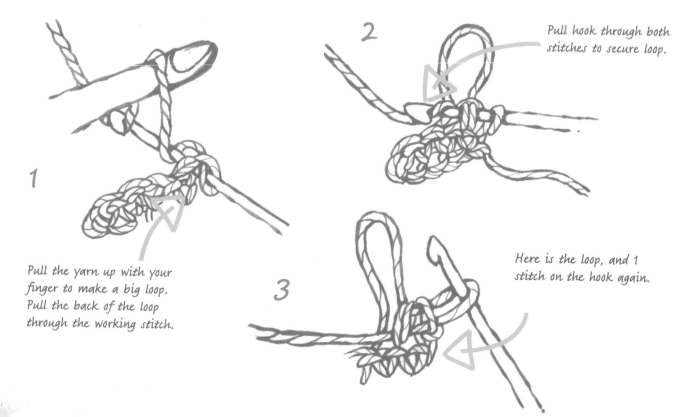

1 Pull the yarn up with your finger to make a big loop. Pull the back of the loop through the working stitch.

2 Pull hook through both stitches to secure loop.

3 Here is the loop, and 1 stitch on the hook again.

EARS (MAKE 2)

Ears are made in dc. Start with 10ch and work in rows of dc, increasing 1dc at the end of each row for 5 rows and then decreasing as you like, depending on the shape of ear your require. The bottom of the ear is folded in half and stitched along the bottom to make the 'pinched' effect of sheeps' ears. Fit them snuggly into the curl of the horn.

You can collect wool from fences when on country walks, then take it home and spin it. See the following pages to learn how.

How to spin

The art of spinning is not lost; it has just be hiding for a while. Once you realise that you can make your own yarn instead of relying on buying it there will be no stopping you. There are many friendly suppliers and websites about pure wool and rare breeds where you can buy the yarn and see what the actual sheep looks like. Contact your local farm and see if they have any fleeces for sale.

Washing fleece

Spinning greasy wool is easier than really clean wool but a dirty fleece can be most unpleasant to handle and you must take care to ensure there are no traces of sheep dip or other chemicals. Half-washing the fleece means it's clean enough to spin but still too oily for dying. The grease makes it a joy to spin and you can wash it clean once it is in a skein.

Pick out all the twigs, burrs and other bits of countryside. Some fleeces have hard lumps of matted wool, so cut those out, there's no point trying to use them. Wash the wool a little bit at a time. Try to choose a warm and windy day to wash the fleece then it will dry more easily. You might know the expression 'hanging on tenterhooks'? This means you are waiting in anxious anticipation, but 'tenterhooks' are actually what you use to hang a fleece or cloth to dry over a 'tenter' or stretching frame.

Carding

Carding is the brushing of fibres before spinning. Hand carders are like big hairbrushes that come in pairs, or you can use a carding machine, where you turn the handle and the fibres are brushed by two brushing drums.

Making a spindle

Sharpen the end of a chopstick into a point. Use that point to stab your way through a small potato. This goes at the bottom – the potato is the weight that makes the spindle spin. Make a notch or hook about 1cm from the other end (it should look like a crochet hook).

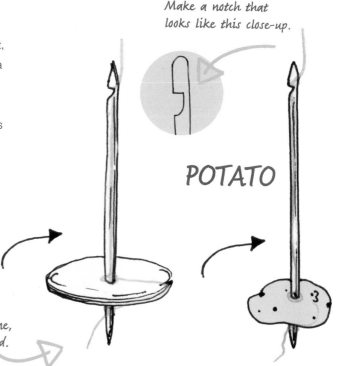

Make a notch that looks like this close-up.

POTATO

This is a proper spindle. If you can get hold of one, it may be more balanced.

Carders are like big
hairbrushes. Pass one
over the other so all the
fibres are lying in the
same direction.

Twist

Spinning can be done clockwise, 'Z' twist, or anti clockwise,
'S' twist. Single threads are usually made with a 'Z' twist, and
if they are folded back on themselves, they twist into a 2-ply
'S' yarn. (See diagram for S and Z.)

Prepare the spindle by attaching a 'leader' thread. This
should be a length of knitting yarn, 'Z' spun. Attach the leader
thread to the notch with a 'snitch knot'. The spindle goes
through the double loop of the snitch knot and then, as the
main thread is pulled tight, the spindle drops and twisted
clockwise, both threads are taken up into the leader thread.
You are now ready to start spinning, clockwise.

All the fibres are being
twisted by the wheel
and turned into thread.

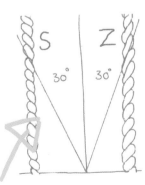

S   Z

30°   30°

The twist can go clockwise or
anti-clockwise, an S or Z twist.

A snitch knot.

Cecilia and
her goats.

SPINNING CONTINUED

To join the fleece, take some combed staple in your hand. Pull some fibres out of the side of the staple. They should overlap each other and be parallel. Lay these fibres out evenly over the last 5cm of the leader thread and hold the thread and fibres tight in your left hand. With the other hand, twist the spindle clockwise and let it drop, until the leader thread is so twisted it kinks.

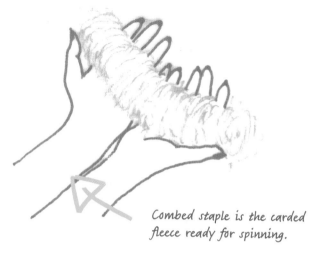

Combed staple is the carded fleece ready for spinning.

Don't make the yarn too twisted or it will kink and be difficult, like this.

Catch the spindle and lay it on your lap; do not allow the yarn to untwist. Now with your left hand, gently allow the twist to move up and take over the fibres resting on the leader thread. They will be sucked into the twist and become secure. Drop the spindle again to make sure they are really twisted. You can help them into the twist by gently rolling them with your hands. Repeat this whole process again.

The basic process is to twist the yarn with the spindle, hold the twist, draft in new fibres, and allow the fibres to be taken over by the twist.

When you have made lots of yarn, you can wind it on! Wind the yarn around the stick and the thread will be secured by the notch at the top of the stick.

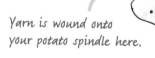

Yarn is wound onto your potato spindle here.

Splicing advice from Cecilia

This is a good way to join in new yarn. It works with wool, mohair and silk. It doesn't work with synthetics.

Unravel a couple of inches of both ends of the yarn that you want to join, not just down to the plies, but to the actual fibres themselves (a needle helps in doing this). Lay the two ends on top of each other and wrap bits of fibre from both ends around each other. Spit on it a couple of times (those of delicate sensibilities might wish to use water, but saliva really is best because of the enzymes). Rub the ends vigorously between the palms of your hands until it is the same thickness as the main body of yarn. Give it a tug to test it's worked.

The Spinning Wheel

Spinning wheels can be found in people's houses as sentimental ornaments. If you discover one of these, pull it out and see if it works. Start by playing with the treadle (pedal) and wheel, push the wheel in a clockwise direction to start and find a regular, slow rhythm. There are many different types of spinning wheel, but here is a diagram that will show you the basics. This is a diagram from a double band wheel. (On a single band, A is next to D.)

The leader yarn will be on the bobbin, and you let the fibres move into the twist the same way you did on the drop spindle. There is more skill required, in that you need to balance the speed of the treadle, the twist of the yarn and the speed you let the fibres in. Once your rhythm is balanced, you can rock the night away and turn fluff into yarn with endless possibilities.

F. Entrance – this is where your thread comes out and your fibres are sucked in. Follow the pink thread on the diagram and see the hole the thread comes out of and into the hooks.

A. The spindle whorl is a little wheel with a groove running through it, which carries the drive band, attached to the main wheel. This wheel makes the spindle turn.

D. Bobbin groove – bobbins have grooves at one end. The bobbin is spinning around and creating a twist to suck in the fibres.

E. There is no E on the diagram. Sorry!

G. Hooks – there are usually 4–5 hooks. These position the thread so you can control on which part of the bobbin, the thread will wind.

C. Break hand tension knob thingy – creates tension between the main wheel and the spindle whorl.

B. The drive band – this is the one piece of string that makes the whole thing happen. It can fall off from time to time and it is very easy to put back on!

No-pop, no-style hat

Don't stay in to wash your hair. Engineer your evening so that your wet locks are cunningly hidden beneath your hat, then you to can get out to those bicycle-maintenance evening classes, with style.

You will need...

YARN: 100g of hand-spun Welsh mountain Aran weight yarn, Colourful oddments in Aran weight

HOOK: 6.5mm

Follow the chart from the centre to the outside. Photocopy this page to make your chart larger if you need to.

Popcorn stitch

STEP 1: After dc, work 5dc into the same stitch.

STEP 2: Remove hook from the working loop and insert from front to back into first dc space and back through original loop.

Key

- ○ chain
- ⊤ treble
- ⬭ popcorn
- ⋎ 2tr in 1st
- ↥ double crochet

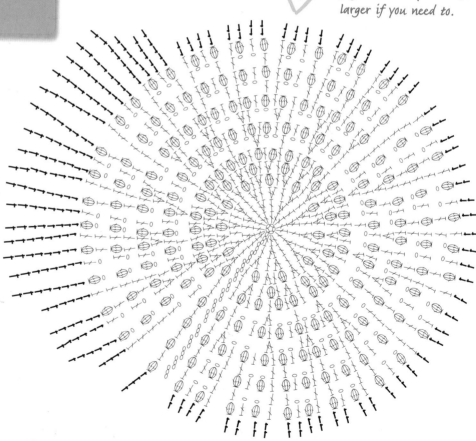

Collar and placket vestee

Whereever you are in the world, you will meet people who love and trust denim. Those familiar shades of blue can make you feel at home anywhere. This soft, blue, flecky cotton yarn is a phenomenon and so is this denim placket collar. A harmonious addition to any wardrobe, it will smarten up any old T-shirt and blend sophistication with casual styling for any morning outing, afternoon tea or evening event.

You will need...

YARN: Rowan denim 100% cotton 93m/50g 1 ball each of 229 Memphis, 225 Nashville and 231 Tennessee

HOOK: 3mm hook

TENSION 6tr per inch (2.5cm). Louise made this collar with exactly one ball of the main colour, so if your tension is looser, you'll need more yarn.

Three shades of indigo dyed denim yarn are used.

Directions

With MC start first half of collar at center back with 17ch.

ROW 1: 1tr in 2nd ch from hook 1tr in each remaining ch (16tr).

ROW 2–10: 1tr in each tr.

ROW 11: Inc (by making 2tr in 1tr), 1tr on each remaining tr.

ROW 12–17: Rep rows 2 and 11 alternately.

ROW 18: As row 2.

ROW 19: Inc 1tr at beginning, 1tr in each remaining tr.

ROW 20: 1tr in each tr, inc 1tr at end.

ROW 21: Inc 1tr at beginning, 1tr in each tr.

ROW 22: As row 20.

ROW 23: Miss 1tr, 1tr, miss 1tr, tr till end.

ROW 24: Tr till last 4sts, miss 1tr, miss 1tr.

ROW 25: Tr, miss 1tr, miss 1tr till 4, then miss 1tr, miss 1tr.

Fasten off, return to centre back of collar then work 1tr into each stitch of foundation ch, complete second half of collar to match first half.

Vestee

LEFT SIDE OF PLACKET AND BUTTONBAND

With MC 40ch.

ROW 1: 1tr in the 4th ch from hook, 1tr in each tr.

ROW 2: 1tr in each tr.

ROW 3: 1tr in each tr, fasten off.

RIGHT SIDE OF PLACKET BUTTONHOLE BAND

ROW 1: Start right side of placket in the same way as left (second row making buttonholes).

ROW 2: 4dtr, * make 2ch miss 2sts, 8dtr * till end.

ROW 3: 1tr in each tr. Fasten off.

Dress up an old T-shirt with a new vestee and some cool glasses, just like Naomi.

Join yarn at top of piece with buttonholes and work into the opposite side of foundation ch.

ROW 1: 5ch, * make a sp (miss 2sts, 1tr in next st, 2ch), rep from * to last st, until 14sps, at the corner of work (1tr, 2ch, 1tr) all into same stitch to turn. Work 3 more sps across lower edge of placket. Now place the other placket strip beneath the one into which you are working, work through both pieces of placket. Turn corner as before, work 2sps up the side, then continue up left side of placket making a further 12sps.

ROW 2: 3ch, 1tr, continue round vestee, 14sps then 3tr at corner, work 4sps across bottom, 3tr at corner, work further 14sps up other side.

At top of right front increase by working 1tr, 2ch, 1tr on last st.

ROW 3: 3ch * 2tr in sp, 1tr on tr below rep from * all round working 4tr into corner sp to turn and increasing once at top edge.

ROW 4: 5ch, miss 2sts * 1tr, 2ch, miss 2sts rep from* till 14sps, 3tr at corner, work 5sps, 3tr, work 14sps, 2tr in last st.

ROW 5: 5ch, 1tr into below tr, 3ch. 1tr into sp below tr, make 14sps then on corner * 1tr, 1ch, 1tr, 1ch, 1tr, 1ch * work 5sps then rep from * to *, work 14 more sps, 2tr in last st. Fasten off.

EDGING

Change yarn to a contrast colour to do last 3 rows.

ROWS 1–2: * 1tr into last tr, work 2tr into space below. Rep from * increasing as required at corner to keep work flat.

ROW 3: Finish with row of picots. Work * 1dc into first tr, 3ch, 1dc in top of dc just made, miss 1tr. Rep from * gauging distance between stitches to make work sit flat.

MAKING BUTTONS

With contrast colour, 4ch join into circle with sl st.

RND 1: work 6dc into circle join with sl st.

RND 2: * (Yoh, hook into circle not into dc round, draw yarn through loosely) 2 times, yoh, draw through all loops on hook, 1ch, rep * 6 times more join with a sl st. 7 petals made.

RND 3: Work 1dc into each st closing petals and 1dc into each ch between petals join with sl st.

RND 4: Work in dc to end.

RND 5: Dec 1dc in every 3rd dc, join with sl st.

Sew buttons on buttonband placket to match buttonholes. Position collar onto vestee and pin and sew when happy with position. Wear and enjoy!

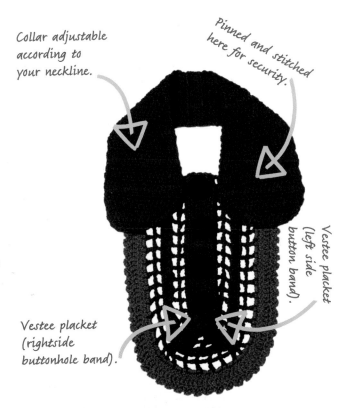

Collar adjustable according to your neckline.

Pinned and stitched here for security.

Vestee placket (left side button band).

Vestee placket (rightside buttonhole band).

Flip-top mittens

Harriet's fingers are always busy making things, even when it's cold. She's invented these detachable-cover mittens, for crocheting in all weather conditions, directing traffic and waving to everyone. UK Alpaca is a super co-operative in Devon that uses British yarns from small herds all over the country, helping to create a viable yarn industry for the farmers involved.

You will need...

YARN: UK Alpaca DK 70% alpaca 30% Bluefaced Leicester Wool, 100g of Sapphire blue

HOOK: 4mm

Just flip the lid over to keep your busy fingers toasty warm.

Directions

CUFF (MAKE 2)

ROW 1: Ch8, 1dc in 2nd ch, 1dc in each ch to end, turn.

ROW 2: 1ch, skip first dc, 1dc in front lp of each dc to end, turn.

ROW 3: 1ch, skip first dc, 1dc in back lp of each dc to end, turn.

Rep rows 2 and 3 until you get to 46 rows.

BACK PANEL (MAKE 2)

Make 25ch.

ROW 1: Skip 4ch * 9tr in next ch, skip 3ch, 1dc in next ch, skip 3ch, rep from * ending in last ch, turn.

ROW 2: 3ch, skip first dc, 4tr tog over next 4tr, * 4ch, 1dc in next tr (centre tr of 9) 3ch, 9tr tog over next (4tr, 1dc, 4tr). Rep from * ending 5tr tog over 5 (4tr, 1ch).

ROW 3: 4ch, 4tr in top of 5tr tog, * skip 3ch, 1dc in dc, skip 4ch, 9tr in top of 9tr tog, rep from * ending in 4tr in top of 4tr tog, turn.

ROW 4: 4ch, skip 1tr, * 9tr tog over (4tr, 1dc, 4tr) 4ch, 1dc in next tr (the centre tr of 9) 3ch, rep from * ending 1dc in 4th of 4ch, turn.

ROW 5: 1ch, skip first dc * skip 4ch, 9ch in top of 9tr tog, skip 3ch, 1dc in dc, rep from * working last dc in first of ch, turn

ROW 6–10: Rep rows 2–5.

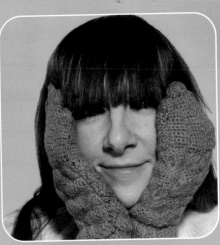

PALM (MAKE 2)

ROW 1: Ch17, 2tr in 4th ch from hook, skip 2ch, 1dc in next ch, * skip 2ch, 4tr in next ch, skip 2ch, 1dc in next ch, rep from * to end. Turn.

ROW 2: 3ch, 2tr in first dc, skip 2tr * 1dc between 2nd and 3rd tr of next group, skip 2tr, *1dc between 2nd and 3rd tr of next group, skip 2tr, 4tr in next dc, skip 2tr, rep from * ending 1dc in sp between last tr and 3ch, turn. Rep until you have 12 rows.

THUMB (MAKE 2)

Ch14, join with sl st.

ROW 1–9: 1ch, 13dc in each ch, join with sl st to first ch. Rep until you have 9 rows (depending on the length of thumb).

ROW 10: 1ch, 7dc into next dc, turn. Rep 15 times, (until row 25). Join yarn at 8th dc on original round, rep row 10, ten times so you end up with a tube with two flaps.

FINGERS (MAKE 4 OF EACH FINGER)

INDEX (PETER POINTER): Ch6, skip1, 1dc in each ch to end. Turn.

ROW 1–18: 1dc in each dc (5) to end.

ROW 19: Skip 2dc, 9tr into dc, skip 1dc, join to last dc with sl st.

MIDDLE FINGER (TOMMY TALL): As for index finger but with 20 rows before last row.

RUBY RING: As for index but with 16 rows and last row.

LITTLE FINGER (PINKIE): As for index but with 12 rows and last row.

MAKING UP

Stitch all the fingers in height order as in the diagram opposite. If the lower edges are very uneven, dc around the base to create a neater edge.

If you are prone to nibble your fingernails then these will suit you.

How to construct mittens

Stitch the fingers together in the right height order.

Fold thumb section leaving flaps open like this.

Assemble the rest of the pieces together like this. Attach the thumb to the main sections, then the cuff around the base.

FLAP

THUMB

CUFF

Harriet likes to wear matching eyshadow with her mittens while she is crocheting.

Schoolboy tie

Love it or hate it, ourschool uniform is the first time we learn to customise and redesign. This school tie will keep you lovely and warm, and blending in with all the other students but enabling you to feel slightly different. This is made with grey alpaca and blue silk in treble stitches, which grow quickly and are easy enough that you can do them under the desk at school or work. Choose colours to match your uniform.

You will need...

YARN: UK Alpaca DK 70% alpaca 30% Bluefaced Leicester Wool, 265m/100g, 50g of grey alpaca (yarn A) Blue sky Alpaca Silk, 50% Alpaca, 50%, 133m/50g in Ice 13 (yarn B)

HOOK: 3.5mm

NEXT ROW: 1tr into each st.

Keep increasing thus every 4 rows until you have 16sts.

Then, keep doing tr without shaping for 12 rows.

Fasten off.

How to construct

Fold along the dotted lines, just like at school...

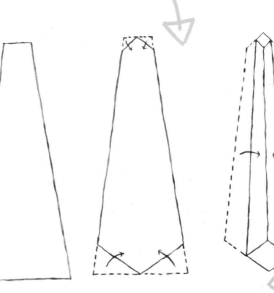

Do you remember doing origami, well this is the same....

Directions

Make 53ch using blue yarn.

ROW 1: 1tr into 3rd ch from hook. 1tr into all sts, make 3ch. Turn. Rep row 1, alternating yarn A and yarn B every two rows to form stripes.

START DECREASING: Maintaining striped pattern throughout, 1tr into first st, 2tr tog over 2sts, 1tr to last 3sts, 2tr tog, 1tr. Make 3ch.

NEXT ROW: 1tr into each st.

Keep decreasing every 2 rows until 12sts are left.

NEXT ROW: 1tr into each st for 40 rows.

START INCREASING: 1tr into first st, 2tr into next st, 1tr to last 2sts, 2tr into next st, 1tr. Make 3ch.

Suitcase cover for a lonely traveller

Never be lonely when travelling alone! So how about taking all your mates along with a photo album suitcase cover. It makes a great talking point with strangers and you can collect more friends for your suitcase on your adventures. Journeys are the best time to crochet.

You will need...

YARN: Colinette Isis 100% viscose, 100g/100m
Oddments of Morocco, Castagna, and Mardi Gras (or any oddments of fancy yarn you find)
DK yarn for the straps, maybe the same colour as your suitcase plus other fancy bits of yarn

HOOK: 4mm

HEADING: 1 suitcase, 30 photos, jam jar, large press studs

Make the holes with a bodkin or big needle, making sure your hook can fit through the holes.

Directions

All suitcases are different so you will need to do your own measuring. For this suitcase the photos were cut into circles 10cm diameter (the size of a large jam jar). Punch holes all the way around each photo, about 1cm from the edge, and about 1cm apart. You can use a large needle or bodkin to do this. Insert hook into first hole from front to back, pull a loop through. * Ch, insert hook into next hole from front to back, pull loop through, ch, sl st. Rep from * to last hole. Insert hook into first st and sl st, finish by tying threads together on WS.

MAKING UP

Using a sewing needle and the same colour yarn, join all the circles together to cover each side of the suitcase. Make two straps in htr crochet to go around full width of suitcase and attach at the top edge with a buckle, bow, or large press stud fasteners.

TIP
This photo album would look great on a messenger bag or briefcase – just resize to fit.

Hot chocolate felting

A chat with Stephen is like having a lovely cup of cocoa, and here he is relaxing with a milk pan at the log cabin. Pure wool is wonderfully practical in the kitchen. It's tough enough to resist heat and flames, keeping your hands safe. It's so durable it doesn't really get dirty, because its complex structure means it doesn't absorb dirt or water, and if there is a large hot chocolate accident, and you do have to wash, then it springs straight back into shape! The coasters are made using patterns for traditional medallion motifs, which you can find in old crochet books in charity shops. They used to be made in fine cotton, for the dressing table, but here they are made in wool and then felted.

You will need...

YARN: Rowan Kidsilk Haze, 70% kid mohair 30% silk 210m/25g ball, 1 x 50g Pearl 590

HOOK: 3.5mm

Don't burn your fingers on the hot milk!

Directions

SAUCEPAN HANDLE

For an average-sized milk-pan handle, start with 14ch, join the last ch to the first with a sl st to form a ring.

RND 1: 2htr tog into first (yo, put hook into next stitch, pull yarn through, rep this action – 5 loops – now pull yarn through all 5 loops). This stitch is quite bobbly, for a firm grip.
* 2htr tog inserting hook in same ch as last st, then in next ch, rep from *. Continue in the round until it is the length of your saucepan handle.

NEXT RND: Decrease, by * miss 1st, and 2htr tog into next ch, rep from * until handle fits snuggly, fasten off and stitch up.

Now make a flowery edging by rejoining the yarn and picking up stitches along the first edge. Insert hook into first ch on chained edge. 4ch, * 4tr tog inserting hook twice in next st, and twice in the following st, 3ch, 1dc in next st, 3ch, rep from * 3 more times, 4tr tog inserting hook as before, 3ch, 1 sl st in first ch of round. Fasten off.

You will need...

MATERIALS: Aran weight Leicester long wool
Tops in different colours for the bases (these are wool fibres that are carded but not spun)
Two pieces of cotton fabric about 4 times the size of the medallion. Washing powder (a bar of soap will do)
A kettle, rubber gloves and elbow grease – I mean muscles and stamina. Good music, with an even tempo

HOOK: 6.5mm

Creamy coasters and placemats

Follow the charts from the centre. Fasten off. Press flat.

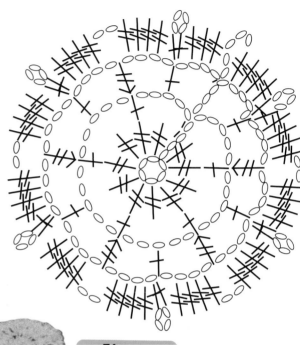

Key

−	slip stitch
○	chain
+	double crochet
‡	treble
↓	double treble

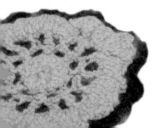

These crocheted medallions were adapted from vintage patterns.

How to felt

1

2

3

4

How to felt your placemat

Most of us have felted by accident when shrinking a favourite woolly jumper in the wash. Wool is one of the few fibres that felts. Felt is not knitted or woven – the fibres link together through friction and heat. Felt is incredibly tough. Conrad of Montferrat had a suit of armour made out of felt during the crusades because he realised that "neither the point of a sword nor even balls discharged from firearms were able to penetrate it". (*The Art of the Felt Maker* by Mary Burkett.) So perfect for coasters.

Directions

1 Boil the kettle.

2 Place a sheet of cotton on a sturdy table. Place your pure wool crochet medallion face down on the cotton sheet. Lay the wool fibres over the top. You can play with the colours at this stage. Colours will show through the crochet, so put them where you want them. Pile layers of fibres on top in a criss-cross formation until it is about 5cm high. Lay the other cotton sheet over the top.

3 Sprinkle soap powder or flakes over the top of the cotton fabric. Pour boiling water into the middle and start rubbing the soap in with your hands. Keep going until everything is saturated and there are loads of soap suds. (You will need to clean the whole kitchen afterwards, as the lather will be everywhere.)

4 Keep working, rubbing the fibres under the cotton fabric. The motion of your hands will make all the fibres stick together. You need to put a good record on and rub the fibres in time to the music, for a good 40 minutes. The longer you rub, the tougher the felt will be. You know when it is ready because the cotton sheet will peel back easily. For extra felting you can bung it in the tumble dryer for 5–10 minutes. The edges will be all wispy and when it is dry you can cut your coasters into shape.

Hula hoop action

Annie's 'special power' is that she can make anything, including most of this book. She is a professional multi-tasker, so we made her lots of bangles for her hula-hoop action. Crocheting around hoops is as easy as winking. Collect bright and fancy yarns and mix them all up to form a superlative outfit.

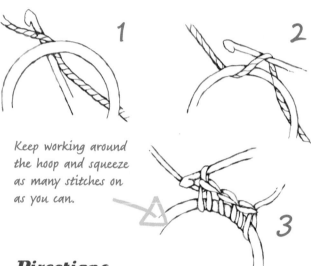

1

2

Keep working around the hoop and squeeze as many stitches on as you can.

3

You will need...

YARN: Use odds and ends to match previous outfits

BANGLES: Original bangles are Indian glass bangles from the market, very cheap (15 bangles for a quid)

HULA HOOPS: Found in back of the garage

HOOK: 3–5mm, depending on size of hoop

Directions

HULA HOOP

Make a chain around the diameter of the tube joining with a sl st. Work 1dc in each chain all the way round the hoop, moving the hook from side-to-side as you go.

EARRINGS

RND 1: Sl st all the way round hoop of metal earring.

RND 2: On the bottom of the earring make 3 scallops (2 small, 1 big) Make the big one first in the middle, then make small scallops either side.

BIG SCALLOP: Sl st, then into same loop, 1dc, 7dtr, 1dc.

SMALL SCALLOP: Sl st, then into same loop, 1dc, 3dtr, 1dc. Fasten off.

PINK KNOBBLER BANGLE

RND 1: Sl st all the way round bangle.

RND 2: * 6 sl st, (dc, 2dtr, dc) all into same st, sl st into next st, rep from *.

BIG CRAZY BRACELET

RND 1: 32 sl st.

RND 2: Dtr in each st.

RND 3: 1ch, tr to end.

RND 4: * 2dc (1dc, 3dtr, 1dc in same hole), rep from *.

Matching earrings.

shady parasol style

modest white lace

Baroque

for delicate hands

order in the court !

Masked ball

This is the glamorous Thelma Spiers, from Hoxton designers Bernstock and Spiers, at a masked ball. Without constant vigilance, masked balls will soon be a thing of the past.

You will need...

YARN: 4-ply cotton in dark navy and pink, plus gold lurex

HOOK: 2.5mm

OTHER MATERIALS: Wire, approx 2 coathangers' worth

Directions

Make 8ch. Join with sl st to first ch to form circle.

RND 1: 1ch to count as first dc, work 15dc into circle. Join with sl st to first ch (16sts).

FIRST SPOKE

ROW 1: 14ch, work 1dc into 3rd ch from hook, 1dc into next ch, work 10dc into the rnd, and not into the ch, 1dc into each of last 3ch, sl st into next dc along the circle, turn.

ROW 2: Work 1dc into each of first 3dc, * 4ch, miss 1dc, 1dc into next dc, * rep 5 times, 1dc into each of next 2dc, 1dc into second of first 2ch. Turn.

ROW 3: 1ch to count as first dc, 1dc into each of next 3dc, * 4dc into 4ch loop,1dc into next dc *. Rep 5 times, 1dc into each of last 2dc, sl st into next dc along the circle, turn.

SECOND SPOKE

ROW 1: Make 13ch, sl st into center st of third loop along first spoke, turn, work 1dc into each of next 3ch, work 10dc around the ch, 1dc into each of last 3ch, sl st into next dc along circle, turn and complete as for first spoke but on next row end with

1dc into each of last 3dc instead of last 2dc and turning ch. Work third spoke in the same way as second.

BIG SPOKE FOR EYE

Make 39ch, sl st into centre st of 4th loop along third spoke, turn, work 1dc into each of next 3ch, work 36dc round the ch, 1dc into each of last 3ch, sl st into next dc along circle, turn and complete as for first spoke but work * 15 times instead of 5 times. Fasten off. Make two symmetrical halves.

JEWELLERY (MAKE 2)

Using yarn loop method and pink yarn, 4dc into circle, join to first dc with sl st.

RND 2: 2dc into all sts. **RND 3:** 1dc into first 2sts, 2dc into next. Rep these to end. **RND 4:** 1dc into each st. **RND 5:** As rnd 4.

RND 6: Change to gold Lurex, 1dc into each st.

RND 7–8: As rnd 4.

RND 9: * 1dc into first 2sts, skip 1dc. Rep from * to end.

RND 10: 1dc into first st, skip next st rep to end. Fasten off.

Thread the wire along the red line.

● WIRE

Parasol edgings and lazy-lace gloves

In ancient Greece, the word for a host and a guest is the same, and here is Jennifer in all her loveliness, welcoming and embracing everyone with hands that enchant in crisp white gloves. She protects her complexion under a parasol that glistens with pearls, ready for the showers that may fall.

Directions
Parasol cover

Starting with yellow yarn, make a yarn loop, 15dc into loop, join with sl st.

ROW 1: Dc into every dc (15sts).

ROW 2: Tr into every dc (15sts).

ROW 3: * Dtr into next tr, 1ch, rep from *.

ROW 4: 2dc into each ch sp.

ROW 5: Change to white yarn,* dtr into next dc, miss next dc, rep from *.

You will need...

YARN: Coats Aida crochet cotton 280m/50g #10 in White and yellow, 1 Parasol or umbrella
Pearl beads for decoration

HOOK: 3mm

ROW 6: * 6ch, miss 2dtr, dc into next dtr, rep from *.

ROW 7: * 6ch, dc into loop, rep from *. Continue this pattern until work measures 15cm. Then work: * 7ch, dc into loop, rep from * until work measures 20cm.

Continue in this way increasing 1ch every 5cm, until the cover fits your parasol/umbrella.

COVER EDGING

Using yellow yarn * dc into the loop (the same number of dc should be worked as the final number of ch you made for each loop), rep from * join with sl st. Next * 8ch, miss 4dc, dc into next dc, rep from *.

PARASOL EDGING

Crochet a number of chains divisible by 4, plus 2 for the required length.

Pretty edgings in contrast colours wherever you fancy.

Key
- • Start point
- ○ chain
- + double crochet
- ✠ treble
- \ slip stitch

Star motif

Start from the middle of the chart and work your way out to the edges.

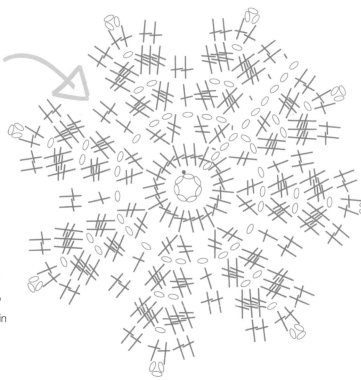

CONTINUED

ROW 1: 1dc into 4th ch from hook, * 1ch, miss 1ch, 1dc into next ch, rep from * to end. Turn.

ROW 2: 2ch, * 6ch, miss 1ch, and 1dc and 1ch of previous row, 1dc into next dc, rep from * to end. Turn.

ROW 3: 2ch, * 3dc into next 6ch loop, 3ch, 1 sl st into side of last dc worked to form picot, 3dc into same 6ch loop, 1dc into dc between loops, rep from * to end. Finish off. Thread ribbon in first row.

STAR MOTIF FOR PARASOL TOP

Starting with yellow, work 7ch. Join into a circle by working a sl st into the first ch (see chart above).

ROW 1: Work 2ch to form first st, work 23dc into circle. Join to 2nd of 2ch with sl st. Break yarn and leave end for darning.

ROW 2: Join white yarn with sl st to top of last st worked, 4ch, 1tr into same st as first st, 1ch, * miss 2dc of preceding round, 1tr, 2ch, 1tr all into next dc, 1ch, rep from * 6 times. Join with sl st into 2nd of first ch.

ROW 3: With same colour, work 2ch, 1tr, 2ch, 2tr, all into first 2ch space of preceding round, 1dc into next 1ch space, * 2tr, 2ch, 2tr all into next 2ch space, 1dc into next 1ch space, rep from * 6 times. Join with sl st into 2nd of first 2ch. Break yarn.

ROW 4: Join in yellow. 2ch, 2tr, 1ch, 3tr all into 2ch space of preceding round, 1dc on each side of dc of preceding round, * 3tr, 1ch, 3tr, all into next 2ch space, 1dc on each side of next dc, rep from * 6 times. Join with sl st to 2nd of 2ch. Break yarn, leaving an end for darning.

ROW 5: Join in contrast colour as before, 2ch, 1dc into each of next 3tr, 1dc, 3ch, 1dc all into first 1ch space, 1dc into each of next 4sts. *1dc into each of next 4sts, 1dc, 3ch, 1dc all into next 1ch space, 1dc into each of next 4sts, rep from * 6 times. Join with sl st into 2nd of first 2ch. Break yarn and darn in all the ends. Press.

Change the colour of your edging to match the flowers in your garden.

Fingerless lacy gloves Directions

Commence with 58ch in white. Join into a ring with a sl st.

ROW 1: * 5ch, miss 2 of the foundation ch, 1dc into ch. Rep from * all round, forming 18 loops.

ROW 2: * 5ch, 1dc in centre of loop, rep from * all round. Rep the 2nd row until 12 rows have been worked in all. Mark the side of the glove with a thread or marker.

THUMB

(5ch, 1dc in next loop) 3 times, then make 12ch, turn back and make 1dc on dc marked by thread. This forms a ring for the thumb. Continue in pattern for thumb on 6 loops, for 3 rows. Break yarn and fasten off.

Now join the yarn where the marked thread is. Carry this thread up with every row so that the position for the first finger is marked. Work 3 loops at base of thumb and continue for 12 more rows.

FINGERS

FIRST FINGER: This is worked on 5 loops. Work the 2 loops to the left of the thread, then make 5ch, work 1dc in 3rd loop from thread at back of glove. Work in pattern for 3 rows. Break yarn and fasten off.

2ND FINGER: Work next 2 loops from front, make 5ch, then work 2 loops from back and make 1 loop at base of first finger (6 loops in all). Work for 3 rows, break yarn and fasten off.

3RD FINGER: As 2nd finger.

4TH FINGER: Work on remaining 4 loops, make 1 loop at base of 3rd finger. Work 2 rows, break yarn and fasten off.

Make the other glove the same way, turning inside out so that the thumb is in the right position.

CUFF

Join yellow yarn at lower edge of glove (foundation ch) and work into the loops.

ROW 1: 2dc into sp of 2ch, 1dc into base of foundation dc, rep from * all round (58dc), join with a sl st.

ROW 2: * 6ch, miss 5dc, 1htr into next dc, 2htr into next dc, rep from * join with sl st.

ROW 3: * 8ch, miss 6ch, 1htr, 2htr into next htr, 1htr into next htr rep from * join with sl st.

ROW 4: * 9ch miss 8ch, 1htr, 2htr into next htr, 1htr into next htr rep from * join with sl st.

ROW 5: * 10ch miss 9ch, 1htr, 2htr into next htr, 1htr into next htr rep from *, join with sl st, break yarn and fasten off.

Rep for the other glove.

FINGER EDGING

Work into the loops in yellow, 3dc into each sp for all finger edges and thumbs.

Science experiment jumper

It's all about experimenting, so be prepared! This is Michael, our lovely work-experience student who experimented with lots of things while we were making this book. Here he is mixing some potions in an alpaca periodic tank top. We all miss him. Katy, our editor, ordered 'Mardi Gras' yarn and we thought she was mad because it wasn't our style at all. Well she was very clever, because it has become the most favourite yarn in this book. Here it is being used for acid spills, something that she constantly battles against because she is the wife of a scientist as well as being a mother and an inspiration to us all.

You will need...

YARN: UK Alpaca DK 70% alpaca 30% Bluefaced Leicester Wool, 265m/100g, 200g of grey (yarn A), 100g of red (yarn C), 100g of blue (yarn D)

Blue sky Alpaca Silk, 50% Alpaca, 50% 133m/50g 50g Ice (yarn B)

Colinette Isis, 100% viscose 100m/100g, 100g Mardi Gras

HOOK: 6mm

MATERIALS: Pattern paper

You can use this fluffy Isis yarn for so many special effects. Get some in your stash.

Directions

This sleeveless top was made to fit Michael and it is 76cm long from the nape of the neck to the base and 91cm around the chest. Sorry it's got no sleeves, they have corroded completely. I suggest you experiment with the pattern of this jumper as follows.

1. Find a jumper that fits, and a piece of pattern paper that is slightly bigger than the jumper (pattern paper or thin see-through paper). Lay the jumper out flat and draw around it as accurately as you can. Take care drawing around the back of the neck. You can draw the V later. Take the jumper away and fold the piece of paper in half vertically down the centre of the pattern. By doing this you can re-draw the shape by taking an average of both sides. Cut it in half with the paper still folded. Your pattern will be symmetrical. Now make the front pattern. Copy the back pattern, fold in half again and draw in your V-neck. The tip of Michael's V is 23cm from the back neck edge. Cut.

Experimental chart

CONTINUED

2. Look up the periodic table on the internet or in your old science folder from school (bet you wish you hadn't thrown it away), and choose which part of it interests you most. I chose the non-metals. Draw out the table on your pattern. Colour in any squares that are a different colour from the main colour. Each square is filled with 9tr, and then 1ch that lies underneath the vertical lines in the table. Vertical lines are made afterwards in colour B using surface chain stitch. Draw on the acid burns too!

3. Start at the bottom of the front. With yarn B, make a chain that is divisible by 10, nearest the width of the pattern plus 3ch. I suggest 73ch.

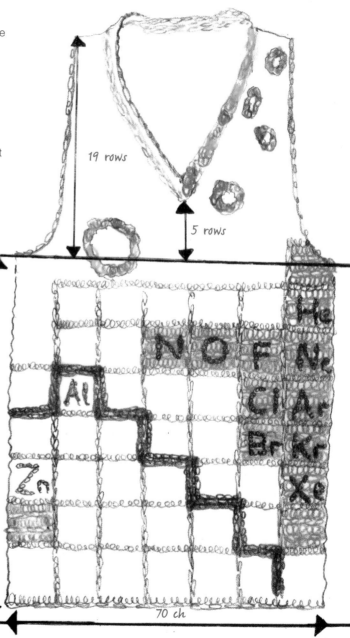

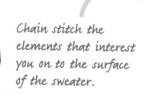

Chain stitch the elements that interest you on to the surface of the sweater.

ROW 1: In yarn B, Skip first 3ch, and * 1tr in each of next 9ch, 1ch, miss 1ch. Rep from * to end.

ROW 2: Change to yarn A or whichever colour your periodic table demands. 3ch, * 9tr, 1ch, rep from * to end.
Rep row 2, four more times. Each row of the table is made up of 5 rows.

ROW 6: Change to yarn B, rep row 2.

ROW 7: Rep rows 2–6 all the way up the periodic table, changing colour as needed. When you get past the periodic table just carry on in rows of trebles. For shaping of the armholes and neck, keep laying your work down on the pattern paper. Michael's armholes appear after 48 rows, dec 2sts at each end of every row for 4 rows. To decrease, form clusters as follows,

STEP 1: Work each of the sts to be joined up to the last 'yrh pull through' that will complete it. One loop from each st to be joined should remain on the hook, plus the loop from the previous st. Wrap the yarn around the hook once again.

STEP 2: Pull a loop through all the loops on the hook. One loop now remains on the hook.

From the beginning of the armhole dec, work 19 rows then shape shoulders by dec 4sts on the armhole edge for 2 rows.

TO MAKE AN ACID BURN HOLE

Just stop wherever you want to form a hole and turn, 3ch, and continue. You can decrease at the edges as the hole goes out. To increase back over the hole, work 2 or 3tr into the tr on the edge. Or form extra ch to fill in the gap. Work up the other side of the hole. When the 2 sides of the hole are even, tr over the chains filling the gap and continue.

To form the edging of the acid burn, use Mardi Gras and sl st around the edge of the hole. To finish, thread the threads through a large bodkin and thread through the acid yarn, pulling the edge tight. This is quite important for keeping the shape of the garment.

The dark surface-crochet lines are added at the end.

The back of the garment is made in rows of trebles in colour A, following the shape of armholes for front. At back neck, stop after 19 rows from armholes and form shoulders to match the front. Place holes wherever you feel the need.

MAKING UP

Join the shoulder seams together. To finish the neck, pick up the sts around the neckline and dc in col A or Mardi Gras. The blue stripe on the neck edge is done in surface ch st, as are the letters and the diagonal lines on the chart. Stitch or hook the side seams together. Experiment complete.

Powdered wig

Wigs were invented for bad hair days. They have the added benefit of keeping you warm, and in the case of this wig, framing the beautiful Annie, fashionable for any period or era in which you find yourself.

You will need...

YARN: Blue Sky Bulky 41m/100g
6 x Polar Bear 1004

HOOK: 3.75mm, 4.75mm and 9mm

Directions

This is a very easy pattern all done in tr. One base strip for head rectangle shape (A). Two large side-curls rectangle shape (B). Two smaller rectangles for top curls (C). Four small rectangle for side curls and small top curls (D).

HEAD-STRIP A (MAKE 1)

Using 3.75mm hook, 28ch.

ROW 1–3: 1tr in each ch (28 tr) till end. Fasten off.

LARGE SIDE CURLS B (MAKE 2)

Use 9mm hook, 30ch.

ROW 1–4: 1tr in each ch (30 tr) to end. Fasten off.

SMALLER SIDE CURLS C (MAKE 2)

Use 9mm hook, 15ch.

ROW 1–4: 1tr in each ch (15 tr) till end. Fasten off

SMALL TOPSIDE CURL D (MAKE 4)

Use 4.75mm hook, 12 base ch.

ROW 1–4: 1tr in each ch (15 tr) till end. Fasten off.

PLAITS

The back of wig hair is made from rows of chains attached to back of head strip. When wig is made up, length of each ch should be approx 30cm leaving a small

Three curls stack up each side to keep your ears really warm.

tail to use when sewing plaits on to wig. Gather at the bottom using a bow.

MAKING UP

Lay head strip flat and sew both pieces of the large side-curl rectangles (B) to each end of head strip (A) to make one long strip. The side curls will be slightly wider than head strip so centre the side curls, then roll up like a swiss-roll. Using a large darning needle sew into position. Roll the smaller side-curls (C) and attach above the big curl (B). Roll the four smaller curls (D). And place one each side on the very top of curls and two on the side of wig in between. Sew long plaits/ch one at a time using the base ch on to the head strip at back. Gather into pony tail and fasten with bow. If you are a knitter, why not make a knitted bow? (See Rachael's other book, *Knitorama* p48; cast on half the number of stitches specified to make a small bow.)

Slip spats

As you fall from grace, as one does from time to time, do it with dignity. These delightfully lacy spats are crocheted in two sections. Here's how to make this necessary accessory to complete any outfit with panache.

You will need...

YARN: Rowan denim cotton 93m/50g
1 ball in 324 Ecru
2m of 4cm wide Black satin ribbon

HOOK: 3.75mm

Each spat is simply made from two crochet motifs that join along the heel and have a strap that slides under the sole.

Directions

Following the chart overleaf, make a circle using yarn loop method and make 10dc into loop.

RND 1: (5ch, miss 1dc, 1dc) 5 times.

RND 2: * Miss 1ch, dc into next 4ch of loop, rep from * last loop, dc in each ch.

RND 3: * 6ch, miss 2dc, dc into next dc rep from *, sl st 2 or 3ch to start next rnd from centre of loop.

RND 4: * 6ch, dc into centre ch of loop rep from *.

RND 5: 4ch, dc into last dc made, 5dc into next space, * 4ch, dc into dc in centre of loop, 5dc into next sp, rep from *.

RND 6: * 10ch, 1dc into middle of sp in last rnd, rep from *.

RND 7: 4 or 5 sl st up side of loop to start from the centre, * 10ch, 1dc into middle of loop in last rnd, rep from *.

RND 8: * 1tr into next 10ch, 3ch, rep from *.

Make four of this piece.

QUARTER: Commence with 7ch, join into loop with sl st.

ROW 1: 5dc.

ROW 2: 5ch, 1dc in next dc, 5ch, miss 1dc, 1dc in next dc, 5ch, 1dc in next dc, sl st into the last 2ch made.

ROW 3: * 6ch, 1dc into the middle of the last loop, rep from *.

ROW 4: (4ch, 1dc into last dc made, 6dc into loop) twice, 4ch, 1dc into last dc made.

ROW 5: * 10ch, 1dc into middle of loop, rep from * twice more.

ROW 6: Sl st into the last 3 or 4ch made, * 10ch, 1dc into the middle of last loop, rep from * once more.

CONTINUED

ROW 7: Tr into every chain (20tr).

Make two of this piece.

UNDER-HEEL STRAP

ROW 1: 6ch.

ROW 2: Miss 1ch, dc in every ch.

ROW 3–6: 5dc, 1ch.

Make two of this piece.

LOOPY EDGING

To make up, follow diagrams then add the loopy edging around all the edges as foll: dc into spat edge, 8ch, miss 3tr, 1dc into next tr. Sew ribbon bow to front.

Key

- • Start point
- ○ chain
- + double crochet
- ‡ treble
- ╲ slip stitch

Spats diagram

This is a quarter segment. Make 2.

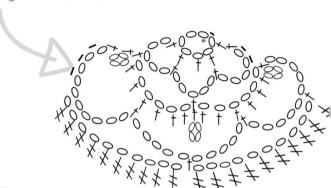

Main motif (make 4).

tch up along the
ck of the heel.

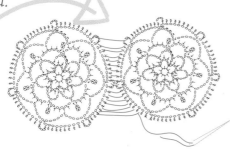

Stitch on the
under-heel strap.

BACK VIEW

Add the quarter
segment at the
front, fitting it
around the shoe.

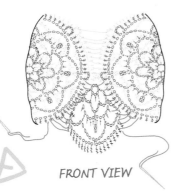

FRONT VIEW

Tunisian Banana

Banana skins are very interesting. They are funny, dangerous and yellow. People joke about bananas, slip up on bananas or just go bananas. This makes a crochet banana skin an interesting accessory to be used in different situations. It can look great pinned on your head or displayed on your car dashboard. Bananas can be found in Tunisia, so this in made in Tunisian crochet. Tunisian crochet doesn't stretch and can be worked in two or more colours. You can make any kind of fruit you want; you just need to experiment.

Remember what your
mother told you about
wearing decent smalls?
Now you know why.

Lacy top with detachable yoke

We adapted this pattern from a garment especially designed for the queen. We prefer it on Amy Higgins. The detachable yoke is for changeable weather conditions. Undo the buttons for a plunging neckline, button up if you feel a draught.

You will need...

YARN: Blue Sky Alpaca Silk 50% alpaca 50% silk 133m/50g 4 x 50g 33 Blush (A). 1x 50g 20 White (B), 1 x 50g 10 Ecru (C)

MATERIALS: Tapestry needle
29 buttons approx 1cm diameter

HOOK: 2.5mm and 3.5mm

TENSION: 1 row = 1cm in V-stitch. Motifs are approx 2cm in width

MEASUREMENTS: Top measures 50cm from shoulder
To fit 34 inch bust

Directions

FRONT

Using 3.5mm hook and yarn A, ch88. Work 16 rows horizontal rib as follows:

ROW 1: 1dc into 2nd ch from hook, 1dc into each of next ch, ch1, turn; 87dc.

ROW 2: * 1dc into the horizontal bar that lies under the normal ch loop at the top of the next dc, rep to last ch 1dc into t-ch, ch1, turn.

Rep row 2 for a further 14 rows, on the last row working 3 t-ch. Change to 2.5mm hook to start V-st main body.

ROW 1 (WS): Miss first bar, (1tr, 2ch, 1tr) into next horizontal bar, 1V-st made, * miss 2dc bars, 1V-st into next horizontal bar, rep from * to last bar, 1V-st, into bar, 1tr into t-ch, 3ch, turn; 29V-sts.

ROW 2: * 1V-st into ch sp in next V-st, rep from * to end, 1tr into turning ch, turn. 29V-sts. Row 2 forms pattern for body, work a further 30 rows as this row. On row 32, do not work any t-ch at end of row.

We had a set, but you can collect little buttons for an eclectic effect.

SHAPING FOR NECK AND ARMHOLES (LEFT)

ROW 33: Sl st along to 3rd V-st, 1ch, 1V-st into 4th V-st, work V-st into each of next 10V-sts, 1 sl st into 1st of next 2ch, turn; 11V-sts.

ROW 34: Sl st along first 2ch sp, 1ch, 1V-st into next V-st, work 1V-st into each of next 8sts, 3ch, turn; 9V-sts.

ROW 35: 1V-st into each of next 7sts, 1 sl st into 1st of next 2ch, turn; 7V-sts.

ROW 36: Sl st along first 2ch sp, 1ch. 1V-st into next V-st, work 1V-st into each of next 5sts, 3ch, turn; 6V-sts.

ROW 37: 1V-sts into each of next 5sts, 1 sl st into first of next 2ch, turn; 5 V-sts.

ROW 38: Sl st along first 2ch sp, 1ch, 1V-st into next V-st, work 1V-st into each of next 3sts, work 1V-st into top of t-ch, 3ch, turn; 5sts.

ROW 39: 1V-st into each st to end, turn; 5sts.

ROW 40: Sl st along first 2ch sp , 1ch. 1V-st into next V-st, work 1V-st in each st to end, work 1V-st into t-ch, 3ch, turn; 5sts.

ROW 41: 1V-st into each st to end, 3ch, turn; 5sts.

ROWS 42–43: As row 41.

ROW 44: 1V-st into next V-st, work 1V-st in each st to end, work one V-st into t-ch, 3ch, turn; 6sts.

ROW 45: 1V-st into each st to end, 3ch, turn; 6sts.

ROW 46: 1V-st into next V-st, work 1V-st in each st to end, work 1V-st into t-ch, 3ch, turn; 7sts.

ROW 47: 1V-st into each st to end, 3ch, turn; 7sts.

Fasten off yarn.

RIGHT SIDE

Attach yarn on unworked opposite side of row 32, working on wrong side, to 2ch of 3rd V-st.

ROW 33: 1ch, 1V-st into 4th V-st, work V-st into each of next 10V-sts, 1 sl st into 1st of next 2ch, turn; 11V-sts.

ROW 34: Sl st along first 2 ch sp, 1ch, 1V-st into next V-st, work 1V-st into each of next 8sts, 3ch, turn; 9V-sts.

ROW 35: 1V-st into each of next 7sts, 1 sl st into 1st of next 2ch, turn; 7V-sts.

Make a carnation for yourself if nobody is going to send you one...

ROW 36: Sl st along first 2ch sp, 1ch. 1V-st into next V-st, work 1V-st into each of next 5sts, 3ch, turn; 6V-sts.

ROW 37: 1V-sts into each of next 5sts, 1 sl st into 1st of next 2ch, turn; 5V-sts.

ROW 38: Sl st along first 2ch sp, 1ch, 1V-st into next V-st, work 1V-st into each of next 3sts, work 1V-st into top of t-ch, 3ch, turn; 5sts.

ROW 39: 1V-st into each st to end, turn; 5sts.

ROW 40: Sl st along first 2ch sp, 1ch. 1V-st into next V-st, work 1V-st in each st to end, work 1V-st into t-ch, 3ch, turn; 5sts.

ROW 41: 1V-st into each st to end, 3ch, turn; 5sts.

ROW 42–43: As row 41.

ROW 44: 1V-st into next V-st, work 1V-st in each st to end, work 1V-st into t-ch, 3ch, turn; 6sts.

ROW 45: 1V-st into each st to end, 3ch turn, 6sts.

ROW 46: 1V-st into next V-st, work 1V-st in each st to end, work 1V-st into t-ch, 3ch, turn; 7sts.

ROW 47: 1V-st into each st to end, 3ch turn; 7sts.

Fasten off yarn. Make the back as front. Sew shoulder and side seams neatly.

MOTIFS

Using 2.5mm hook and yarn B, work 9ch, join with sl st to first ch to form ring.

ROW 1: * 1dc into ring, 4ch, rep from * 5 times more, 1 sl st into first dc, 6 petals. Fasten off.

Work next motif as first motif but do not bind off. Attach by inserting hook into 3rd ch of a petal of previous motif and pulling loop through both this and last ch on hook of next motif. Bind off. Attach 26 following motifs in the same way.

Sew motif chain neatly along neckline, ensuring the central ring of each motif is free (overhanging the neckline).

Make two 12-long motif chains and attach to each armhole, omitting the underarm shaping.

Make a further 16-long motif chain for the yoke.

YOKE

Using yarn C and 3.5mm hook, ch179.

TR2TOG (TREBLE 2 TOGETHER): * 1 tr into next chain but leaving last loop on hook (stopping before last yoh), rpt from * in next stitch, then yoh and draw through all 3 loops (1 stitch has been decreased).

ROW 1: Work 1 tr into 4th chain from hook, 1tr into each of the next 19 ch, * (tr2tog) twice (2sts decreased), 1tr into each of next 40ch, rpt from * 3 times more (total of 8sts decreased), 1tr into each of next 20ch, 6ch, turn; 168sts.

ROW 2: * Miss 3tr, 1dc into next tr, 5ch, rep from * ending with 1dc into top of t-ch, 5ch, turn.

ROW 3: * 1dc into next loop, 5ch, rep from * ending with 1dc into 3rd of t-ch, 5ch, turn.

ROWS 4–5: * 1dc into next loop, 4ch, rep from * ending with 1dc into 3rd of t-ch, 4ch, turn.

ROWS 6–9: * 1dc into next loop, 3ch, rep from * ending with 1dc into 3rd of t-ch, 3ch, turn.

ROWS 10–14: * 1dc into next loop, 2ch, rep from * ending with 1dc into 3rd of t-ch, 2ch, turn.

ROW 15: Work 2tr into each 2ch space, to end. Fasten off.

Attach the 16-long motif chain around the top of the yoke, leaving the last motif overhanging one end to act as buttonhole fastening. Attach one button to centre of last motif at opposite end of yoke. Sew 28 buttons on to the bottom of the yoke to correspond with the centre rings of the motifs around the neckline of main body. Use these motifs to button the yoke in place.

glamorous gloves for the glitterati

Black for Night Time

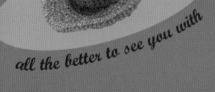

all the better to see you with

put your feet up and read

Fancy-that gloves

Here is Louise wearing a dramatic new look, the lacy night-time gloves. They make you feel so fancy that you will find yourself going out on rave dates in one glove while you finish the other.

You will need...

YARN: Coats crochet cotton Eldorado 50g 265m/50g in black. 1.5m of Satin 5cm wide ribbon white or cream

HOOK: 1.75mm

MEASUREMENTS: To fit an average 6.5 to 6.75 hand

Directions

Commence with 58ch. Join into a ring with a sl st.

ROW 1: * 5ch, miss 2 of the foundation ch, 1dc into ch. Rep from * all round, forming 18 loops.

ROW 2: * 5ch, 1dc in centre of loop, rep from * all round. Repeat the 2nd row until 12 rows have been worked in all. Mark the side of the glove with a thread.

THUMB

(5ch, 1dc in next loop) 3 times, then make 12ch, turn back and make 1dc on dc marked by thread. This forms a ring for the thumb. Continue in pattern for thumb, on 6 loops, for 9 rows. Shape top as follows.

NEXT 2 ROWS: Work 4ch, 1dc in centre, then in next row, work 3ch, 1dc and in next row 2ch, 1dc; break yarn, draw up top of thumb and fasten on wrong side.

Now join the yarn where the marked thread is. Carry this thread up with every row so that the position for the first finger is marked. Work 3 loops at base of thumb and continue for 12 more rows.

FINGERS

FIRT FINGER: This is worked on 5 loops. Work the 2 loops to the left of the thread, then make 5ch, work 1dc 3rd loop from thread at back of glove. Work in pattern for 10 rows, then shape as thumb.

2ND FINGER: Work next 2 loops from front, make 5ch, then work 2 loops from back and make 1 loop at base of first finger; 6 loops in all. Work for 12 rows, then shape top as thumb.

3RD FINGER: As 2nd finger, but for 10 rows only.

4TH FINGER: Work on remaining 4 loops, make 1 loop at base of 3rd finger. Work 9 rows only, shape top as in thumb.

Make the other glove to match Turn inside out so that the thumb is in the right position.

CUFF

Join yarn at lower edge of glove (foundation ch) and work into the loops.

ROW 1: 2dc into sp of 2ch, 1dc into base of foundation dc rep from * all round (58dc), join with a sl st.

ROW 2–3: Dc every dc.

LOOPS

32ch, miss 6dc, 1dc into next dc, 13dc in the last 13ch made, * 19ch, miss 6dc, 1dc into next dc, 13dc in the last 13ch made, rep from *, join to 13th ch made.

NEXT 2 ROWS: Dc all the outer ch, break yarn and fasten off.

Baguette and knee warmers

Nick has peddled like mad in these indispensable knee warmers to pick up the fresh bread from Mark's patisserie before his lover awakes and needs her breakfast. Mark assures us the baguettes will stay warm all the way home in these red, white and blue 100% machine washable baguette warmers.

You will need...

YARN: Sirdar Double Crepe DK 270m/100g 55% acrylic 45% nylon. 1x 100g each colour: 242 Flamenco (yarn A), 273 Royal (yarn B), 251 white (yarn C)

HOOK: 4mm

Directions

The baguette warmers are made in a tube of double crochet and the knee warmers are in crochet rib.

Begin with red yarn (A), use the yarn loop method to make a circle and 7dc into the circle.

RND 1: Join first dc and last dc together with sl st, 1t-ch.

RND 2: 1dc into first dc, 2dc into every dc from previous round, to end.

RND 3–4: * 1dc into first dc, 2dc into next dc, rep from * to end.

RND 5: * 1dc into each of next 3dc, 2dc into next dc, rep from * to end.

RND 6: * 1dc into each of next 4dc, 2dc into next dc, rep from * to end.

RND 7–12: 1dc in every dc to end.

The rounds will start to form a cylinder shape. Change colour every 5 rounds, and continue until it is the required length for your baguette.

If you know your baker well, you'll know what size his loaves will be.

Knee warmers

Make your knees stand out in a crowd with these eye-catching kneepads. Use them over the top of your skateboarding pads for that go-faster look. Failing that, they are good for polishing floors.

Directions

THE SHAPED PIECE: Make 2ch.

ROW 1: Miss 1ch, 3dc into next ch, 1ch, turn.

ROW 2: Inc by working 2dc into first st, 1dc into next dc, inc 1ch, turn.

NEXT 11 ROWS: Inc, then 1dc, in every st till 1 rem, inc, 1ch, turn.

ROW 14: 4dc, (inc, then 5dc) 3 times, inc, then 4dc, 1ch, turn.

NEXT 4 ROWS: 31dc, 1ch, turn.

ROW 19: 4dc, (dec, by working 2dc tog, then 5dc) 3 times, dec, 4dc, 1ch, turn.

ROW 20–31: Miss first st, then 1dc in every st till 2 rem, 1ch, turn.

ROW 32: 3dc tog, fasten off.

Stitch these in your national colours.

THE RIBBING: Make 37ch.

ROW 1: Miss 1ch, 1dc into each of next 36ch, 1ch, turn. Work into top back thread of every st to give ribbed effect.

NEXT 7 ROWS: 36dc, 1ch, turn.

ROW 9: 18dc, leave rem 18dc unworked, then take shaped piece and sl st into end of each of first two rows worked, turn.

ROW 10: Miss the 2 sl st then 18dc on 18dc, 1ch, turn.

ROW 11: 18dc, then sl st into each of next 2 rows on shaped piece, turn, rep last 2 rows 14 times, then rep 10th row. Join ribbing to other side of shaped piece thus: use second ball of yarn and sl st into opposite end of first row on shaped piece, then work 18dc on the 18dc left unworked in the 9th row, 1 ch, turn, rep 11th and 10th rows respectively 15 times.

NEXT ROW: 18dc, sl st to end of next row on shaped piece, fasten off. Return to first ball of yarn, work 18dc on first side, then 18dc on other side making a continuous row 36dc long, 1ch, turn.

NEXT 6 ROWS: 36dc, 1ch, turn.

LAST ROW: Dc to end, fasten off. Sew up back seam.

Sparkling neckline

It's a treat to be neat, and here is Louise ordering her paperwork in a dramatic choker.
A mix of lazy hemp and busy beads, these sophisticated accessories make neckline news.

A scrap of soft leather makes a good tie.

You will need...

YARN: Natural fine hemp from The House of Hemp, 100% hemp, 340m/50g

HOOK: 2.5mm

MEASUREMENTS: Choker: 3cm x 22cm
Glasses chain: 98cm x .5cm

OTHER MATERIALS: 20g 4mm hematite crystal bicones (approx 200 beads for choker, 100 for glasses chain). Scrap of leather or suede, big-eye beading needle, eyeglass grips

Directions

Thread all the beads for the choker onto the thread all at once.

ROW 1: 10ch, turn.

ROW 2: Miss 2ch, work dc across row to end. 1ch, turn.

ROW 3: RS, work dc to end, 1ch, turn.

ROW 4: WS (beading row) – pull a bead up to the hook. Begin to make dc. As you bring yoh, pull a bead up and pull tight within stitch so it sits at the back of the work. Repeat this in each dc to end of row, 1ch, turn.

ROW 5: Work dc to end, 1ch, turn.

Repeat rows 4–5 eighteen times.

Without fastening off, work a single chain of 30sts incorporating a bead every alternate stitch. Sl st to the bottom edge of the choker about halfway along, then continue with another slightly shorter chain. Attach towards far end of choker about 6 rows from edge. Sl st to the end and ch40 To make a dropper, make a chain of 9 including beads, turn leaving 3 beads at end, and work back up the chain with sl sts. To make further chains, sl st along the bottom edge and make chains and drops until your beads run out. We worked three chains and three drops but you can do as much as you can with the remaining beads.

Cut two strips of leather or soft material approx 32cm long and the same width as the choker. Sew on to the ends of the choker. Trim strips so they narrow to a point at ends for ease of tying.

GLASSES CHAIN

Make a chain of 3, turn.

ROW 1: Miss first st, 2dc along row, 1ch, turn.

ROW 2: Work 2 beads into this row.

Repeat rows 1 and 2 until 34cm worked. Work plain dc without beads for 27cm (so the beads aren't scratchy around the neck). Resume beading every alternate row until whole chain measures 98cm or desired length. Work a row through the loop of the eyeglass grips at both ends. Fasten off.

Lonely lampshade

At Halloween I had a party and Miranda came as a standard lamp. She was dressed entirely in black with a fancy lampshade on her head. The female body is a bit like the shape of a traditional turned lamp base. Here is a pattern for a lampshade, crocheted with a broomstick, in-keeping with Halloween, the one night of the year where you want to shine in the darkness; or just put it on a normal lamp base like this one.

You will need...

YARN: Debbie Bliss Pure Silk, 100% silk, 125m/50g approx 5 skeins in Cream 04

BROOMSTICK: 35mm broomstick or wooden spoon

HOOK: 4.5mm

MEASUREMENTS: This pattern fits lampshade with top circumference 89cm, bottom circumference 183cm, top edge to bottom edge 41cm

Directions

PANELS (MAKE 4)

Make a dc chain of 48sts.

ROW 1: Pull up 48 loops onto the broomstick through the back loops only of the dc side of the starting chain. Work the loops off the broomstick in groups of 4 loops with 4dc per group (12 groups, 48dc).

ROW 2: Pull up 48 loops. Work off in groups of 4 loops, with 4dc per group (12 groups, 48dc).

ROW 3: As row 2.

ROW 4: Pull up 48 loops. Work off in groups of 4 with 5dc per group (12 groups, 60dc).

ROW 5: Pull up 60 loops. Work off in groups of 5 with 5dc per group (12 groups, 60dc).

ROW 6: As row 5.

dc chain

CHAIN SIDE

DC SIDE

TIP

Dc chains don't get in a twist, and neither does Cecilia. It is easier to count the sts and to work into them. The chain side can look a bit messy but it is an ideal base for an edging.

ROW 7: Pull up 60 lps. Work off in groups of 5 with 6dc per group (12 groups, 72dc).

ROW 8: Pull up 72 lps. Work off in groups of 6 with 6dc per group (12 groups, 72dc).

ROW 9: Pull up 72 lps. Work 6dc in the first 3 lps and 6dc in the next 3. Then work off in groups of 6, with 6dc in each group until 6 lps are remaining on the broomstick. Work 6dc in the next 3 lps and 6dc in the last 3 lps (14 groups, 84dc).

ROW 10: Pull up 84 lps. Work off in groups of 6 with 6dc per group (14 groups, 84dc).

ROW 11: Pull up 84 lps. Work off as per row 9 (14 groups, 84dc).

ROW 12: Pull up 96 lps. Work off in groups of 6 with 6dc per group (16 groups, 96dc).

ROW 13: Pull up 96 lps. Work off as per row 9 (18 groups, 108dc).

ROW 14: Pull up 108 lps, Work off in groups of 6 with 6dc per group (18 groups, 108dc).

ROW 15: As row 14.

MAKING UP: Once you have made four panels in total, join them using small stitches in the ends of the dc ridges; don't pull the thread too tight but let it flow alongside the loops between the ridges. To join seam, thread the tail on to your trusty tapestry needle, make a little stitch through the dcs on both edges, all the way up the edges. Do not pull the thread tight but let it flow with the loops between the dcs. Secure it at the top with a couple of small stitches on the wrong side. Now work the top of the lampshade cover, using the unused loops from the chain side of the dc starting chain. Work an edge in backwards dc (or corded edging, see page 28), working over a long tail end of the thread. Fit the cover over the lampshade and check the fit.

TIP
Make a lovely fringe of tassels to hang down under your lampshade.

Our old lamp stand is a bit broken but it looks better now.

You will need...

YARN: Debbie Bliss Pure Silk, 100% silk, 125m/50g, approx 1 skein in Cream 04

HOOK: 4.5mm

MATERIALS: Various sizes of broomstick from 8mm to 20mm (wooden spoons, knitting needles, broomsticks etc). Lampshade approx 10cm in height

Notes on designing your own lampshade cover

All lampshades seem to be different and the world is awash with spare ones. This pattern can be adapted in various ways. Start by making swatches, using different yarns, and sizes of broomstick. Use different numbers of loops in each group and dcs to work off the groups. Your group of loops should be about 2cm, which makes it easier to work out how big to make your lampshade cover. There are a few ways to increase the size of your work, as the size of the lampshade increases:

1. Use larger broomsticks.

2. Add an extra dc to each group, which will give you more loops on the next row.

3. Work double the number of dcs at the beginning and end groups of a row by dividing those groups in half but working to the same number of dcs in them as the other groups in the row. (For example, if a usual row consists of groups of 6 loops with 6dc in each group, then on the 'increase' row, the first, second, penultimate and ultimate groups should have 3 loops with 6dc in each). A combination of these methods have been used in the making of these lampshades.

Small lonely lampshade

Make a dc chain of 60sts.

ROW 1: Pull up 60 lps through the back of the lp of the dc side of the ch, on to 8mm broomstick.

Work the lps off the broomstick in groups of 3 lps with 3dc in each group (20 groups, 60dc).

ROW 2: Pull up 60 lps on to 10mm broomstick. Work off in groups of 3 lps with 3dc per group (60dc).

ROW 3: Pull up 60 lps on to 12mm broomstick. Work off in groups of 3 lps with 4dc per group (80dc). (Remember there is one more dc than there are lps in each group. It is very easy for the fingers to do the wrong number before the brain catches up!)

ROW 4: Pull up 80 lps on to a 12mm broomstick, work off in groups of 4 lps with 4dc per group (80dc).

ROW 5: Pull up 80 lps on to 15mm broomstick (at this point Cecilia was using a wooden spoon). Work off in groups of 4 lps with 5dc per group (100dc).

ROW 6: Pull up 100 lps on to 15mm broomstick. Work off in groups of 5 lps with 5dc per group (100dc).

ROW 7: Pull up 100 lps on to 20mm broomstick. Work off in groups of 5 lps with 6dc per group (120dc).

Fasten off, leaving 20cm tail.

To join seam, thread the tail on to your trusty tapestry needle, make a little stitch through the dcs on both edges, all the way up the edges. Do not pull the thread tight but let it flow with the loops between the dcs. Secure it at the top with a couple of small stitches on the wrong side.

Now work the top of the lampshade cover, using the unused loops from the chain side of the dc starting chain, work an edge in backwards dc (sometimes known as crab stitch), working over a long tail end of the thread. Fit the cover over the lampshade and check the fit. If the top needs tightening, pull the tail that you crocheted over until the top fits snugly.

"Do not disturb" book cover

Rosie has a thirst for knowledge and her reading time is very precious. That's what makes her an interesting friend and a champion at crossword puzzles. This cozy siesta stunner crocheted in Welsh mountain wool hand-spun by our friend Sue. The gold leaf is with lurex and the little red letters are made with crochet cotton.

Directions

FRONT AND BACK

Make 29ch to start.

ROW1: 1tr into 3rd ch from hook, 1tr in each ch to end, 3ch.

Keep working thus for 26 rows. Fasten off.

Make 1 more for back.

SPINE

Make 9ch to start. 1tr into 3rd ch from hook, 1tr in each ch to end. 3ch. Keep working 1tr without shaping for 26 rows. Fasten off.

Put three parts (front, back and spine) together (see making up illustrations overleaf).

INSIDE

Pick up stitches from each edge.

1dc all round, make 1ch, turn, 2dc tog over next 2 sts, 1tr to last 3sts, 2dc tog, 1dc. Keep decreasing thus for 3 rows. Fasten off.

INSIDE STRAP (MAKE 2)

Make chains long enough to run between top and bottom.

1dc into every chain. Fasten off.

Sew the straps on the inside from top flap to bottom flap.

You will need...

YARN: 100g of Aran weight wool (we used Welsh mountain sheep yarn), 1 ball of gold lurex, oddment of red cotton

HOOK: 4mm

Pick up the stitches and add your favouri *edging (see page 29).*

CONTINUED

DECORATION

See illustrations. However, this is only a suggestion from us.
You can make this book cover into any type of book you want
to pretend that you are reading.

Making up

Sew them together like this,
making chains and flaps to hold
the book in place.

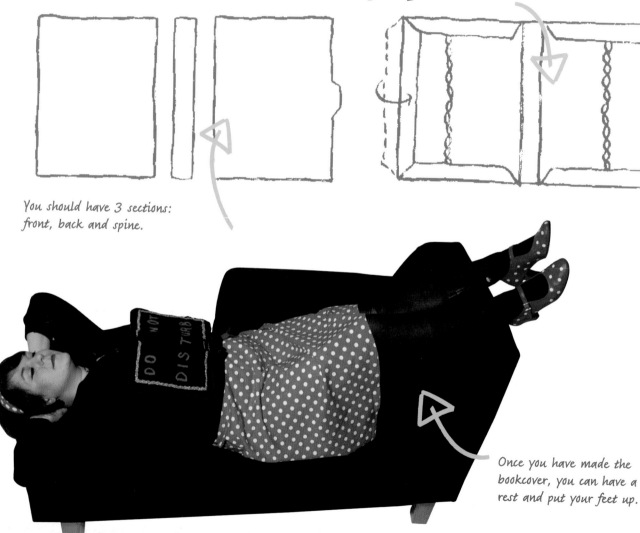

You should have 3 sections:
front, back and spine.

Once you have made the
bookcover, you can have a
rest and put your feet up.

Typeface for bookcover

Use surface crochet to make the lettering in red or gold.

Follow the arrows and work in that direction. Plan out the letters using dressmaker's chalk before you begin.

A candle for the dark

Bring a little light into someone's life with this crochet candle. Please do not ever fall asleep with a candle burning, even if you are burning the proverbial candle at both ends to finish the crochet projects in this book. Cotton candles are much more practical as they neither set fire to things nor drip wax and may still attract beautiful moth species to the flickering illuminations.

You will need...

YARN: Pure cotton yarn in double knit
1x 1oz (25g) ball in colour A, oddment in B, plus gold lurex

HOOK: 4mm

Directions
Brass candlestick

CUP

Using gold and starting at centre bottom, make a yarn loop, 8dc into the ring joining with sl st. Make 1ch.

RND 2: 2dc in each dc, join with sl st. Make 1ch; 16sts.

RND 3: * 1dc into the first st, 2dc into next st. Rep from * eight times, join with sl st. Make 1ch, turn; 24 sts.

RND 4: Working in back loop only, dc in sl st, dc in each of next 23sts, join with sl st. Make 1ch; 24sts.

NEXT 4 RNDS: Dc in each st, join with sl st, make 1 ch. At the end of 8th rnd, turn; 24sts.

RND 9: Working in back loop only, dc in sl st, dc in each of next 23sts, join with sl st. Make 1ch; 24sts.

RND 10: 1dc in each st, join. Fasten off.

SAUCER

RND 1: Holding cup with open end facing you and working in free loops of rnd 3 insert hook in the sl st for joining, draw through a loop, 1ch, dc in same st, dc in each of next 2sts, 2dc in next st, * dc in each of next 3sts, 2dc in next st, rep from * 5 times, join, 1ch; 30sts.

Use red mohair for the flame to make a bigger glow.

RND 2: 1dc in first st, * 2dc in next st, dc in each of next 4sts, rep from * 5 times, 2dc in next dc, 1dc in each of last 3sts, join. 1ch; 36sts.

RND 3: * 1dc in each of next 5sts, 2dc in next st, repeat from * six times, join, 1ch; 42sts.

RND 4: 1dc in each of next 2sts, * 2dc in next st, dc in each of next 4sts, join, 1ch; 48sts.

RND 5: 1dc in each st, join, 1ch; 48sts.

RND6: * 1dc in each of next 11sts, 2dc in nest st, rep from * 4 times, join, 1ch; 52sts.

NEXT 2 RNDS: Work in back loops only: dc in each st, join, 1ch.

RND 9: * 1dc in each of next 11sts, skip next 2sts. Repeat from * 4 times, join; 48sts. Finish off, leaving enough yarn for sewing. Fold 8th and 9th rnd against 5th and 6th rnd leaving 7th rnd as a rim. Whipstitch the edge of 9th rnd to underside of 4th rnd.

HANDLE

10ch, join with sl st to form ring, 1ch, work 22dc into ring, join. Finish off, leaving enough yarn for sewing. Place ring against side of saucer and sew it on. (You can also dc round a cardboard ring and sew it on.)

Candle

Make 23 chs, 1dc into the first ch to form a ring.

RND 1: 1dc in each ch.

Keep working on dc in rnd to half height desired.

Start making wax dripping action thus: * insert hook into the st which you want to have drip, pull the yarn through loop, yoh rep from * into the same st 4 or 5 times, yoh, pull yarn through all loops on hook. Make 1ch to complete.

You can make wax drips any position you like working in dc up to the height required.

NEXT RND: Dc in each of next 15sts, 1ch turn.

NEXT RND: Skip first st, 1dc in each of next 12sts, sl st in each of next 2sts, 4chs to begin first drip. 2dc into the 2nd ch from hook sl st into 2sts left. Continue this way, putting big wax drips anywhere you like. Fasten off.

CANDLE TOP

Make 2 chs.

RND 1: 7dc in 2nd ch from hook.

RND 2: 2 dc in each st.

RND 3: * 1dc in next st, 2dc in next st, rep from * 7 times. Fasten off, leaving enough yarn for sewing in.

FLAME: With red yarn, make 3ch, join with sl st make 1ch.

NEXT RND: 2dc into each st.

NEXT RND: 1dc into first 2 sts, 2dc into next st rep to end.

NEXT RND: 1dc into first 3sts, 2dc into next st rep to end.

NEXT 3 RNDS: 1dc into each st.

NEXT 2 RNDS: 1dc into first st, skip 1 st. rep to end.

Fasten off. Sew flame on to the candle top.

MAKING UP

Place candle top inside rim of candle tube and sew in place, taking needle under both loops of dc on top. Put the cardboard tube inside the candle tube.

Moth

Pure wool lovers know that the yearly fight with the moth is an ongoing problem. Stop losing the battle and work with the moth instead. Making moths is quick and easy and you can place them over or next to the holes on your lampshade or splattered on your car windscreen. Collect little scraps of yarn and make them all night long.

WING (MAKE 2)

Using brown, make 13ch.

ROW 1: Skip 2ch (counts as 1dc), 1dc into each of next 3ch, 1tr into each of next 4ch, 1dc into each of next 4ch, turn.

ROW 2: 1ch (counts as 1dc), skip first st, 1dc into each of next 3sts, 1tr into each of next 4sts, 1dc into each of next 4sts, turn.

ROW 3: Change colour. 3ch (count as 1tr), skip 1 st, 1tr into each of next 3sts, 1dc into each of next 4sts, 1tr into each of next 4sts, turn.

ROW 4: As row 3.

ROW 5–6: As row 2.

ROW 6: Change colour. Make 3ch, 1tr into each of next 8sts, 2tr tog, 1 tr, turn.

ROW 7: 1ch, 2dc tog, 1dc into next 8sts, turn.

ROW 8: 1ch, 1dc into next of 5sts, 3dc tog, 1dc, turn.

ROW 9: 1ch, 2dc tog, 1dc into next of 5sts, turn.

ROW 10: 1ch, 1dc into next of 3sts, 2dc tog, 1dc, turn.

ROW 11: 1ch, 2dc tog, 1dc into next of 3sts, turn.

ROW 12: 1ch, 1dc into next st, 3dc tog. Fasten off.

Make 1 more but do the decreasing on the other side to make wings symmetrical.

BODY

Use the same colours as wings (brown and white).

With loop method, 5dc into the ring, joining it with sl st.

You will need...

YARN: Moth coloured cotton tweed (brown)
Cotton in white, plus oddments for decoration

HOOK: 3mm

NEXT ROW: 2dc into each st.

NEXT ROW: * 1dc into each of next 3sts, 2dc into next st. * Rep from* to * till end.

Keep 1dc into each st in round changing colour randomly until the work is 6cm long, finishing with brown.

NEXT ROW: 1dc into each of next 3sts, skip 1, rep to end.

NEXT ROW: 1dc into each of next 2sts, skip 1, rep to end.

NEXT ROW: 1dc into first st, skip 1, rep to end. Fasten off.

MAKING UP

Sew wings onto the body. Using a scrap of yarn, decorate the wings. (Check your illustrated encyclopedia and do research into moth pattern variations.)

Raid your stash for fluffy, moth-like yarns to decorate your moths.

Those pesky conversions

The shortened words in a crochet pattern are really there to prevent laborious repetition and, of course, to make the patterns shorter and easier to follow. Special abbreviations that are used are mentioned on each pattern page, but these are the main ones that you will encounter in this book.

Abbreviations

[ ]	work instructions within brackets as many times as directed	dc	double crochet	rbtr	raised back treble crochet (1tr in back of stem)
( )	work instructions within parentheses as many times as directed	dc2tog	double crochet 2 stitches together	rem	remain/remaining
*	repeat the instructions following the single asterisk as directed	dec	decrease/decreases	rep	repeat(s)
		dtr	double treble	rf	raised front
		fl	front loop(s)	rfdc	raised front double crochet (1dc in front of stem)
		foll	follow/follows/following		
		g	gram	rfdtr	raised front double treble crochet (1dtr in front of stem)
**	repeat instructions between asterisks as many times as directed	htr	half treble crochet		
		htr2tog	half treble crochet 2 stitches together	rftr	raised front treble crochet (1tr in front of stem)
		inc	increase/increasing		
alt	alternate	lp(s)	loops	R	round or row
approx	approximately	m	metre(s)	rnd(s)	round(s)
beg	begin/beginning	MC	main colour	RS	right side
bet	between	mm	millimetre(s)	sk	skip
bl	back loop(s)	oz	ounce(s)	sl st	slip stitch
bo	bobble	p	picot	sp(s)	space(s)
CC	contrasting colour	patt(s) or patt	pattern(s)	st(s)	stitch(es)
ch	chain stitch	pc	popcorn	tch or t-ch	turning chain
ch	refers to chain or space previously made	pm	place marker	tbl	through back loop
		prev	previous	tog	together
ch-sp	chain space	rb	raised back	tr	treble crochet
CL	cluster	rbdc	raised back double crochet (1dc in back stem)	trtr	triple treble crochet
col	colour			WS	wrong side
cm	centimetre(s)	rbdtr	raised back double treble crochet (1dtr in back stem)	yoh	yarn over hook
cont	continue				

Hook conversions

Welcome to the kooky world of hook sizes. The letters and numbers may vary, so if in doubt, and you probably will be, the metric sizes are the only ones that you can check with a tape measure. Your knitting needle gauge will also work for the metric sizes so you can convert those lovely vintage patterns. Good luck.

Basic information

US	UK
fingering	4-ply
sport	double knit
bulky	chunky

Crochet

US	UK	
sl st	sl st	slip stitch
ch	ch	chain
sc	dc	U.S. single crochet = UK double crochet
dc	tr	U.S. double crochet = UK treble
tr	dtr	U.S. treble = UK double treble

TIP
This page will be useful if you like to buy patterns while on holiday, or in jumble sales.

Crochet hooks

US	METRIC	OLD UK
	2	14
B-1	2.25	
	2.5	12
C-2	2.75	
	3	11
D-3	3.25	10
E-4	3.5	9
F-5	3.75	
G-6	4	8
7	4.5	7
H-8	5	6
I-9	5.5	5
J-10	6	4
K-101/2	6.5	3
	7	2
L-11	8	0
M/N-13	9	00
N/P-15	10	000
	12	
P/ Q	15	

I'm sure Adam and Eve didn't have to worry about these things.

Yarn credits

Thanks to the following for supporting our venture by sending us lots of lovely yarn.

UK Alpaca

Vulscombe Farm

Vulscombe Lane

Cruwys Morchard

Tiverton, Devon EX16 8NB

Tel 01884 243 579

enquiries@ukalpaca.com

www. ukalpaca.com

CLOVER EURO GmbH

Kontor 4 EG, Högerdamm 39

20097 Hamburg

Germany

Tel +49(0)-40-219065-0

Fax +49(0)-40-219065-29

info@clovereuro.de

www.clover-euro.de

Purlescence

Beautiful accessories and bags online

31 Hexham Gardens

Isleworth

Middlesex, TW7 5JR

Fax 0870 7059924

www.purlescence.com

sales@purlescence.co.uk

Blue Sky Alpacas, inc

Luxurious alpacas and organic

cotton yarns.

PO Box 387, St Francis, MN 55070

United States

Tel 888-460-8862

Fax 763-753-3345

info@blueskyalpacas.com

www.blueskyalpacas.com

The House of Hemp

Beautifully dyed range of hemps on

the internet.

Beeston Farm,

Marhamchurch

Cornwall, EX23 0ET

Tel 01288 381 638

tj@thehouseofhemp.co.ukwww.thehouse

ofhemp.co.uk

Rowan Yarns

Green Lane Mill

Holmfirth, HD9 2DX

Tel 01484 681881

Fax 01484 687920

www.knitrowan.com

Cast Off knitting club
has been awarded this
badge of honour.

Designer Yarns Ltd.

Beautiful yarns from Debbie Bliss and
Noro, among others.

Unit 8–10 Newbridge Industrial Estate
Pitt Street, Keighley, West Yorkshire
BD21 4PQ
Tel 01535 664222
Fax 01535 664333
jane@designeryarns.uk.com
www.designeryarns.uk.com

Coats Crafts

Patons yarns, Coats crochet cottons
and Anchor yarns.

Coats Crafts UK
PO Box 22
Lingfield House, Lingfield Point
McMullen Road, Darlington
County Durham DL1 1YQ
consumer.ccuk@coats.com
www.coatscrafts.co.uk

Other exciting places to look for yarn, wherever you are:

Hand Weaver's Studio

29 Haroldstone Road
London, E17 7AN
handweaversstudio@msn.com
Tel 020 8521 2281

Loop

Knit Salon
41 Cross Street
Islington
London N1 2BB
020 7288 1160
info@loop.gb.com
www.loop.gb.com

Lenarow Ltd

Arts and Crafts
169 Blackstock Road
London, N4 2JS
020 7359 1274
www.woolsandcrafts.co.uk

Farmers

Sheep are archetypically placid. Knitters
and hookers radiate peace and so do
sheep. Sheep give us wool to make
things that make us happy, and while we
are crafting, we can realise that human
intelligence and compassion can triumph
over fear and greed, that terror and war
can give way to discussion and peace.
Make sheep not war. (Adapted from a
statement by Randy Sklaver, Sweden.)

• Southdowns wool, hand spun by
Mrs Sue Thomson of Holt Valley Farm,
Clayton, Sussex.
• Welsh Mountain sheep spun by
Mrs Sue Russel of 'Wool and Boat co.'
• Millspun Coloured Lincoln Longwool
from the Tardbigge flock of Mr and Mrs
S. Higgins.
• White Lincoln Longwool from the
Hugenot and Pelham flocks of Mr and
Mrs Wilson.

Acknowledgements

Making a book is never a one-person operation, and this one in particular has been the focus of frenzied activity by many lovely friends, hooking, editing and writing patterns. A huge thank you to everyone who was involved. This has been truly a collective project. (Thanks to Sebastian for pictures of shoot.)

The photographer at work.

Naomi oversaw the proceedings in Fairisle fashion.

Erssie does some last minute stitching.

Helpful hookers

Katy Bevan Sparkling neckline choker, ongoing patience and the biggest job of all: being the editor.

Annie Doi Fig-leaf bikini, banana skin, oranges, pineapple bag, eye mask, sheep, candle, baguette warmers, grapes, moth, book cover, illustrations, immense dedication.

Naomi Johnstone Lacy gloves in white and black, parasol edging, tea set, knee warmers, snakes, bangles and hula-hoops, sheep, slip spats, and immense dedication.

Cecilia from Woolclip.com Pomegranate, grapes and lampshades, plus wonderful chats.

Diana Matthews Lampshade tassels, picture research.

Louise Harris Collar, wig and calming influence.

Harriet Vine Flip-top mittens, moral support and colourful legs.

Rosie Wolfenden Periodic element embroidery, steak dinner, and moral support.

Erssie Knits Lily of the valley flowers, blackberries, leaves, daisies, pattern writing and meticulous checking.

Techan School tie.

Maki Nakamura Book cover and flowers.

Miriam Zadik-Gold Bangles and earrings.

Mary Nazareth Daisies and vines for Daisy fascinator.

Rachael Matthews Daisy fascinator, No-pop no-style hat, Science experiment jumper, grapes, sheep.

Dr Bryson Gore Thanks for the chemistry equipment and inspiration to crochet chemical burns.

Monty Matthews Research.

Michael Lots of this and that.

Angus Leadley Brown Photography.

Peta Grapes.

Clare Montgomerie Detachable yoke top (from behind the counter in Loop).

Models

Amy Higgins from Tatty Devine

Stephen Fowler aka Nervous Stephen

Nick Phillips cyclist extraordinaire

Mark Pawson aggressive school of cultural workers

Jennifer of 'Hot Breath Karaoke'

Jo Zeitlin and Mia Gubbay aren't they lovely?

Michael what work experience?

Harriet and Rosie of Tatty Devine

Ayako Doi (Annie)

Louise Harries of Hoxton Boutique

Thelma Spiers of Bernstock and Spiers

Claire Montgomerie lovely hands for steps

Naomi Johnstone our in-house angel also drew the beautiful circular pattern charts.

The editor in the background.

Michael experiencing his first photo shoot.

Reviewing the progress.

Annie didn't want to be the princess, so she chose Rumplestiltskin.

Index